IBERO‑AMERICANA:35

NEW SPAIN'S
CENTURY OF DEPRESSION

WOODROW BORAH

NEW SPAIN'S
CENTURY OF DEPRESSION

BY

WOODROW BORAH

UNIVERSITY OF CALIFORNIA PRESS
BERKELEY AND LOS ANGELES
1951

IBERO-AMERICANA: 35

Editors: C. O. Sauer, G. P. Hammond, J. H. Rowe, L. B. Simpson
58 pages, 1 figure
Submitted by editors September 27, 1950
Issued June 28, 1951

University of California Press
Berkeley and Los Angeles

❖

Cambridge University Press
London, England

ACKNOWLEDGEMENT

A NUMBER of people have generously assisted me in preparing this paper. François Chevalier of the Institut Français d'Amérique Latine in Mexico City kindly allowed me to consult the manuscript of his fine study on the formation of latifundia in New Spain. Sherburne F. Cook and Lesley Byrd Simpson, whose striking study of central Mexican population in the sixteenth century furnished the springboard for my interpretation of the movement of colonial Mexican economy, have discussed at length with me the meaning of their investigations and possible extension of them into other fields. Lesley Simpson, further, has served as thorough though sympathetic critic. Carl O. Sauer generously permitted me free use of his remarkable collection of photographs of Spanish manuscripts. Finally, I thank George Kubler and the Yale University Press for permission to reproduce the series of graphs showing building activity by monastic orders in New Spain from *Mexican Architecture of the Sixteenth Century*.

CONTENTS

NEW SPAIN'S CENTURY OF DEPRESSION

INTRODUCTION

IN THIS paper I shall interpret the movement of Mexican colonial economy in terms of demographic findings. I shall indicate that from 1576 until well over a century later New Spain had a contracting economy. Further, this long period of depression was a major factor in molding the Mexican land and labor systems which became dominant in the seventeenth century and remained so down to the Revolution of 1910. My interpretation is obviously a hypothesis which needs much additional investigation.

Historians have tended to assume that New Spain had a continuously expanding economy. That interpretation can be briefly summarized. During the sixteenth century the European conquerors grafted a new economy upon the Indian base which they found in the central areas of present-day Mexico, and eventually European and Indian techniques were fused in a mestizo culture which was and remains distinctively Mexican. During the seventeenth century New Spain slowly reached higher quantitative levels of production within the areas of early conquest while colonial authority was extended northward over the present northern Mexican states and our State of New Mexico. In the eighteenth century the colonial economy continued to expand at an accelerating rate at the same time that Spanish rule was established over more than half the present area of the United States.

The effect which this interpretation has had upon the treatment of data is strikingly illustrated in the calculations of Mexican mining output by the noted nineteenth-century scholar, Adolf Soetbeer.[1] For the period 1521–1587 Soetbeer had a list of shipments of treasure to Spain; for the period 1690 to the end of the colonial period, he had the surviving Mexico City mint figures as reported by Alexander von Humboldt. For the one-hundred-and-two-year period 1588–1689 inclusive, he had no data whatever. On first treatment of the data available, Soetbeer found with concern that his calculations gave him a production figure for 1587 that was higher than calculated specie output for New Spain in 1690. Rather than accept a figure which ran directly counter to the prevailing idea of the movement of New Spanish economy, he at once concluded that his method was wrong and arbitrarily adjusted all his calculations for the sixteenth century sharply downward. He then arranged estimates for the one-hundred-and-two-year gap to show a slow,

---

[1] See pages 47–58, for notes.

steady rise in output throughout the sixteenth and seventeenth centuries until the relatively reliable calculations based upon the mint statistics beginning with 1690.[2] Agreement with the same idea of steady if gradual expansion in the colonial Mexican economy was so general that Soetbeer's contemporary, W. Lexis, who subjected these calculations to severe and even hostile examination, accepted Soetbeer's formulation of general trend in mining output without discussion.[3] Soetbeer's calculations, incidentally, are still reproduced without question in the official Mexican *Anuario Estadístico*.[4] Nevertheless, as the present paper will indicate, Soetbeer's calculations were nearer the mark before he adjusted them to conform to the prevailing conception of the trend of the colonial economy.

The interpretation that the colonial Mexican economy had a continuous if gradual growth has been based, I suspect, upon studies of territorial expansion. For Mexico, the colonial period did indeed show almost continual acquisition of territory, although at a fluctuating rate. Demographic research, however, indicates that a steady upward trend, if postulated for the movement of Mexican colonial economy, would have run directly counter to population movement during most of the colonial period.

DECLINE OF THE INDIAN POPULATION AND ITS EFFECTS ON INDIAN ECONOMY

In recent years investigations have given us a much clearer idea of the movement of Mexican population during the colonial period. Investigators by and large agree that at the time of the Conquest there was a relatively dense aboriginal population in central Mexico; that thereafter this population declined by reason of exposure to new diseases, disruption of native economy, and poor living conditions under the post-Conquest regime.[5] Miguel O. de Mendizábal, after examining sixteenth-century summaries of the answers to royal tax and census inquiries, postulated an average Indian natural family of 3.2 for the middle decades of the sixteenth century.[6] Since the birth rate probably remained fairly constant in a population lacking widespread knowledge of contraceptive measures, an average family of this size presupposes so high a continuing death rate, infant, child, and adult, that the population could not have been maintained at equilibrium. Even without the factor of epidemic disease, therefore, the Indians were gradually but steadily declining in numbers.[7] The great epidemics, such as those of 1545–1546 and 1576–1579 brought catastrophic drops in this general downward trend.

A monograph by Cook and Simpson (1948) based upon examination of tribute rolls and population counts for the sixteenth century and upon the viceregal census of 1790–1793 arrived at the population estimates for central Mexico listed in table 1. Their figures for 1540–1607 are for Indians alone and hence ignore the presence of small numbers of persons of other races and mixed-bloods; estimates for 1650–1793 are for total population.[8] These figures point to: (1) a sharp initial decrease in Indian population under the shock of the Conquest; (2) a period of relative stability between the two

TABLE 1

POPULATION OF CENTRAL MEXICO, ACCORDING TO COOK
AND SIMPSON

Year	Total population
1519	app. 11,000,000
1540	6,427,466
1565	4,409,180
1597	app. 2,500,000
1607	2,014,000
ca. 1650	1,500,000
1700	app. 2,000,000
1793	3,700,000

great epidemics of the 1540's and the 1570's during which the downward movement slackened so that it would be shown on a graph as a gentle slope; and (3) thereafter, a sharp decrease through the rest of the sixteenth century and the early half of the seventeenth century. The low point would appear to have occurred in the middle of the seventeenth century at the bottom of a long shallow trough on the population graph. Cook and Simpson assign a value of 1,500,000 to the total central Mexican population at this low point. By then mixed-bloods, Negroes, and whites were elements of demographic importance, numbering together perhaps 300,000. The Indian population *ca.* 1650 was thus approximately 1,200,000.

Demographic recovery began toward the end of the seventeenth century. It meant at first a slow and then a relatively rapid rise in numbers. By 1793 the total population of central Mexico was perhaps 3,700,000, approximately two-and-one-half times the value for *ca.* 1650 but only four-fifths of the Indian population in 1565.

Recovery involved a substantial change in the racial composition of the population. Whereas the decline occurred among the Indian majority, the recovery was due, more largely, to increase in the number of non-Indians and mixed-bloods. During the latter part of the seventeenth century and the early part of the eighteenth, demographic recovery was due, probably entirely, to increase among the last two groups, whereas the Indian population remained relatively stable or may even have decreased slightly. Only by the middle decades of the eighteenth century did Indians clearly begin to increase although always at a lower rate than the mixed-bloods and non-Indians.[9] As a result, the ratio of the Indians to whole population continued to shrink, so that today Mexico is a mestizo rather than an Indian country.

The large mixed-blood element, which developed in the later colonial period and speeded up demographic recovery, would show a relatively steady upward trend if its growth were charted separately on a population graph. The Indians would show precipitate and prolonged decline from 1519 with recovery beginning only in the eighteenth century. The demographic trend for total population was a decline from 1519 to perhaps the last quarter of the seventeenth century and then partial recovery at a gradually accelerating rate.

The figures in table 1 indicate beyond question that contraction must have taken place at least in the Indian economy of central Mexico as distinct from the economy associated with the European conquerors. Until we possess detailed studies of the effects of this population decline upon the Indian economy, any comments are mere surmises, but we may guess that the economic contraction was nearly, though not quite equal, to the decline in Indian numbers. The new techniques and crops introduced by the Spaniards would have increased Indian production wherever the natives adopted wheeled vehicles, the plow, winter cereals permitting growing two crops a year, and domestic animals for clothing, food, and traction, and the resulting greater efficiency in production would have tended to counteract in the effects of the decrease in numbers of workers. It is doubtful, however, that the adoption of European techniques, animals, and crops could have increased efficiency of production to make up more than a small fraction of the loss because of depopulation. Moreover, during the colonial period a large proportion of the natives probably continued to use pre-Conquest crops and methods. Some improvement in crop yields also would have resulted from the contraction of the cultivated area, since the Indian villages would tend to retire marginal land from production and concentrate crop-raising upon their better and more easily worked soils. Again, the differential gain from this retirement of poorer areas from cultivation was probably small as against the decrease in production because of loss of workers. Any tendency for a proportionate increase in the working capacity of the population because the sturdier adults would have a lower death rate than children, aged, and the weak was probably balanced by enfeeblement among the survivors of disease. It seems likely, therefore, that during the sixteenth and seventeenth centuries the Indian villages progressively lost productive power proportionately to and probably nearly equal to the decrease in the number of their inhabitants.

We may safely postulate further that the contraction of the Indian economy was accompanied by a decrease in the demands upon production from within the Indian villages. Reduction in Indian numbers meant automatic reduction in the number of mouths which had to be fed. On the other hand, the heavy demands upon the villages for the support of their local officials, community activities, and the large class of Indian nobles probably failed to decrease at a rate equal to the decline in the general Indian population. Village governments and religious cults had to be maintained regardless of the number of inhabitants.[10] Similarly the Indian nobility, being better fed and housed, would show a somewhat lower death rate in the epidemics than the mass of Indian commoners. The burden upon the general Indian population which support of nobles and community activities represented therefore probably became proportionately heavier as the villages shrank in size. In consequence, the ability of the Indian villages to contribute to the support of the new European segment of the population introduced by the Conquest was reduced not only by the sharp curtailment in their production but by greater pressure from within Indian society itself upon the remaining output of food and services.

THE MOVEMENT OF WHITE POPULATION

Obviously the disappearance of so much of the Indian population also affected the economy of the European segment of the population. To estimate the nature and extent of the effect, however, we must first gain an idea of the demographic movement of the new upper stratum which the Conquest imposed upon the Indian base. Unfortunately, there exists as yet no usable study of the development of the Spanish elements in the Mexican population during the colonial period; it thus becomes necessary to construct a series of estimates here to obtain the data necessary for comparison.

At the outset, it should be made clear that the upper stratum, although commonly called Spanish, included small numbers of immigrants from most countries of western and central Europe.[11] Further, although considered completely white racially, this stratum contained a very large number of mestizos, bred of the intermarriage of white males and Indian women who were reared as Spaniards and assimilated completely into the European group.[12] After the first generation of white migration, it may well be that a majority of the so-called Spanish were really mestizos.[13] Nevertheless, the group regarded itself and was regarded as Spanish. It remained distinct from the Indians in economy and culture, and functioned as a European and dominant segment of the population.

Further, a comment on method. During the colonial period, writers and royal officials counted Spanish population in terms of heads of families, or *vecinos*. Vecinos, the equivalent of the English term "burghers," should have meant adult males admitted to citizenship in one of the Spanish towns, but in practice it was applied to any adult male Spanish settler of such position that he would have been eligible for citizenship in a Spanish town, for many Spanish settled in Indian towns and villages where they could have no citizenship.[14] In order to convert the number of Spanish vecinos into total population, it must be multiplied by a factor sufficient to take into account women, children, and unenfranchised or dependent Spaniards. A factor of five is frequently used as the size of the natural Spanish colonial family; that is parents and their children.[15] This figure may be too low, since with the high death rate prevailing in those centuries even among the well-to-do, a natural family of five would have meant a population barely maintaining its numbers rather than one on the increase.[16] To take into account, in addition, relatives, employees, servants, and other dependent white persons attached to the household, it is necessary to calculate the average size of the social family; that is, the natural family together with relatives and dependents of whatever category forming the household. A factor of six seems conservative, since colonial households tended to be large, especially in Mexico City and other administrative centers, and many of the Spanish vecinos employed numbers of unenfranchised white men as foremen and managers on their farms and other enterprises.[17] The number of Spanish vecinos multiplied by a factor of six therefore will be the basis for estimating the number of the lay white population. To this figure must further be added a calculation for the clergy—ecclesiastical dignitaries, parish priests, friars, monks, and nuns—who formed a substantial group in the colonial white population. The result will be an estimate of the size of the so-called white stratum in the colonial population.

In 1521, when Tenochtitlán fell to Cortés, the new white element numbered only the men in the Spanish army. During the following decades the white element grew rapidly as new immigrants came from Europe and other Spanish possessions in the New World and as the settlers began to rear families. After the first years, natural increase probably became by far the more important factor in population growth.

The earliest relatively comprehensive estimates for the Spanish population of New Spain available at present are for the years 1569–1571, half a century

TABLE 2

STATED TOTALS OF SPANISH VECINOS IN BISHOPRICS OF NEW
SPAIN, ACCORDING TO LÓPEZ DE VELASCO

Bishopric	Vecinos	Page references in López de Velasco
Mexico....................	2,794	187
Puebla....................	400	207–208
Oaxaca....................	420	227
Michoacán.................	1,000	240
Nueva Galicia.............	1,500	262
Total New Spain..........	6,114	

after the Conquest. They were prepared in answer to an order from the Spanish crown for a series of reports on the population, revenues, and resources of its dominions in New Spain. During the years 1571–1574 these estimates were summarized by the royal cosmographer-chronicler, Juan López de Velasco.[18] Table 2 lists the number of Spanish vecinos given by López de Velasco for each of the bishoprics of New Spain proper. By New Spain proper is meant the administrative areas of the Audiencias of Mexico and Guadalajara exclusive of the provinces in the bishopric of Yucatán, which were considered a special administrative unit. Chiapa was included in the Audiencia of Guatemala so that New Spain in these terms meant the areas from the Isthmus of Tehuantepec north to the limits of Spanish occupation.

Table 2 gives a grand total of 6,114 Spanish vecinos for New Spain proper. A careful reading of the text of López de Velasco, however, discloses serious discrepancies in these figures, for they do not agree with totals arrived at by adding together his figures for towns and districts. For example, López de Velasco lists 2,794 Spanish vecinos for the archbishopric of Mexico, yet he

TABLE 3

LOCAL ESTIMATES OF SPANISH VECINOS IN NEW SPAIN, ACCORDING TO LÓPEZ DE VELASCO

Area	Vecinos[a]	Variant estimates	Page references in López de Velasco
Archbishopric of Mexico			
Mexico City	3,000	...	
Teotlalpan Province	...	130	194
Mines of Pachuca	90	...	196
Ixmiquilpan	50	...	
Pánuco Province	...	60	197
Pánuco	10	...	198, 200
Valles	11	...	200
Tampico	24	16	
Huejutla	20	...	199
Ojitipa	11	...	200
Toluca	200	90	200–210; 187
Sultepec Province	...	200	200–201
Mines of Temascaltepec	60	...	202
Mines of Sultepec	200	...	
Texcoco	60	40	187
Chalco Province	30	...	203
Cuernavaca	5	...	204
La Coixca Province	...	160	205
Mines of Zacualpan	70	...	205–206
Mines and district of Tasco	100	...	
Acapulco Province	...	...	
Coyuca	50	...	
Total	3,991		
Bishopric of Puebla			
Puebla	500	...	209–210
Tlaxcala	50	...	
Atlixco Valley	1,000	...	
Ozumba Valley	800	...	210–211
Tepeaca Province	300	...	
Tecamachalco	200	...	
San Pablo Valley	100[b]	...	
Veracruz	200	...	212
Total	3,150		
Bishopric of Oaxaca			228
Oaxaca (Antequera)	350	...	
Villa Alta (San Ildefonso de los Zapotecas)	30	...	230–231
Nejapa	?	...	
Coatzacoalcos (Villa de Espíritu Santo)	?	...	
Tehuantepec	?	...	
Total	380		

TABLE 3—Continued

Area	Vecinos[a]	Variant estimates	Page references in López de Velasco
Bishopric of Michoacán			
Patzcuaro (Ciudad de Michoacán later moved to Valladolid)	100	. . .	241–244
Guayangareo	30	. . .	
Mines of Guanajuato	600	. . .	
San Miguel	20	. . .	
San Felipe	20	. . .	
Zacatula	15	. . .	
Colima	30	. . .	
Total	815		
Bishopric of Nueva Galicia			
Guadalajara Province	. . .	250	265
Guadalajara	150	. . .	266–267
Santa María de los Lagos	30	. . .	
Mines of Huauchinango	30	. . .	
Mines of Jocotlán	?	. . .	
Mines of Huajacatlán	20	. . .	
Mines of Cuitlapilco	25	. . .	
Compostela	20	. . .	268–271
La Purificación	12	. . .	
Jerez de la Frontera	12	. . .	
Mines of Zacatecas	300	. . .	
Mines and district of San Martín	400	. . .	
Mines of Sombrerete (Villa de Llerena)	?	. . .	
Mines of Chalchihuites	?	. . .	
Nombre de Dios	30	. . .	
Durango	30	. . .	
Chiametla	13	. . .	275–277
Culiacán	30	. . .	
Nueva Vizcaya Province	?	. . .	
Sinaloa	?	. . .	
Total	1,102		
TOTAL NEW SPAIN	9,438		

[a] Wherever there is a discrepancy between the total given by López de Velasco for a province and the sum of the estimates for settlements in the province, the estimates for settlements have been used in the main table and the estimate for the province listed as a variant.

[b] The passage from which these estimates are taken is one of the more obscure in López de Velasco, and may involve duplication although the description covers the series of large, open valleys with good plow land from Puebla to Tepeaca. "Valle de Oçumba. En comarca de esta tierra, siete leguas de la ciudad [Puebla] al oriente, esta el Valle de Oçumba, donde hay más de ochocientos españoles, estancias y ganados, y en la provincia de Tepeaca, cinco leguas al oriente de la ciudad, declinando al sur, habrá más de trecientos españoles, en ganados, grangerias y oficios. Hay en esta provincia un pueblo de indios, ciudad que llaman *Tepeaca*, cabeza de toda la provincia, á quien Don Hernando Cortés llamó *Segura de la Sierra* por estar metida en una sierra; y en esta comarca hay un pueblo de indios que llaman *Tecamachalco*, en que habrá doscientos españoles y más de diez mil indios; cuya comarca, aunque esta es tierra seca, es fértil de mucho maíz, y está en su jurisdiccion el *valle de San Pablo* muy fértil de trigo y en que habrá más de cien españoles labradores."

gives 2,700 Spanish families for the much smaller province of Mexico[19] and 3,000 Spanish vecinos for the even smaller city of Mexico.[20] Similarly, the Spanish population of the city of Puebla (500 vecinos)[21] is larger than the total assigned to the entire bishopric of Puebla. It is possible that some of the discrepancy arose because López de Velasco eliminated duplication; that is, a vecino of Mexico City owning a farm in the valley of Atlixco, bishopric of Puebla, might have appeared in the counts for both places, but such an explanation does not easily fit a reading of the text, nor can it account for the discrepancies in the estimates for the archbishopric, province, and city of Mexico or those for the city and bishopric of Puebla. Accordingly, the district and town figures given by López de Velasco have been listed in table 3 and totaled by bishopric.

Table 3 gives a grand total of 9,438 Spanish households. The totals for the archbishopric of Mexico and the bishopric of Puebla in table 2 are substantially higher than the corresponding totals in table 1. Those for the bishoprics of Oaxaca, Michoacán, and Nueva Galicia are lower, but the lower values are easily explained by the fact that estimates are not given for all the Spanish settlements in those dioceses. For example, examination of what was probably López de Velasco's source for statistics on the bishopric of Oaxaca discloses that the discrepancy of 40 vecinos in table 3 lies in the unlisted population of the two Spanish settlements of Villa Alta and Nejapa, each of which in 1570 had 20 vecinos.[22] With an allowance for these settlements, the total of table 3 for the bishopric of Oaxaca would be 420, the value of table 2. This total is probably still too low, since it makes no allowance for Tehuantepec or Coatzacoalcos, both of which in 1570 had a number of Spanish families settled at the ports and on near-by farms.[23] Nevertheless, the figure is the best estimate evailable at this time. Accordingly, in table 4 the estimates for the bishoprics of Oaxaca, Michoacán, and Nueva Galicia in table 1 have been substituted for the totals of table 2 in order to take into account Spanish settlements in those dioceses for which data are not given by López de Velasco. It should be emphasized that these estimates cannot be considered maxima, since counting in frontier areas was much more subject to errors of omission than counting in the more accessible and better settled central dioceses of Mexico and Puebla.

The grand total of table 4 is 10,061 Spanish vecinos in New Spain proper *ca.* 1570. Multiplied by six, this gives a lay population of 60,366.

The estimate for the clergy must represent an extension of López de Velasco's data. He states that the number of clergy in the province of

Mexico alone was in excess of 1,000.[24] The province of Mexico as the area of heaviest concentration of both secular and regular clergy probably had less than half but rather more than a quarter of the clergy of the entire colony. Hence 2,500 would seem to be a conservative value for the five bishoprics. This figure, added to that for the lay white population, gives a total white population of 62,866 for New Spain proper in 1570, or to round the number, since it is a crude calculation at best, 63,000.

The area of this estimate is somewhat larger than the area covered by the calculations for Indian population in Cook and Simpson. A value of

TABLE 4

ADJUSTED TOTALS FOR SPANISH VECINOS IN NEW SPAIN,
ACCORDING TO LÓPEZ DE VELASCO

Bishopric	Vecinos
Mexico	3,991
Puebla	3,150
Oaxaca	420
Michoacán	1,000
Nueva Galicia	1,500
Total for New Spain	10,061

6,000 would seem to be a reasonable allowance for the sparse Spanish settlement in Querétaro, Guanajuato, northern Zacatecas, most of San Luis Potosí, Nueva Vizcaya, Nayarit, and Sinaloa; thus the Spanish population of central Mexico in 1570 was approximately 57,000. This total should be compared with the Cook and Simpson estimate of 4,409,180 for Indian population in 1565.

Three-quarters of a century after López de Velasco prepared his compendium, a second secretary attached to the Council of the Indies prepared another compendium or description of the Spanish dominions in America. Spain by then had developed a disproportionately large bureaucracy, and so the secretary was primarily interested in official positions and salaries available in each town, who held them, and how appointment was secured; but he did excerpt some estimates of white population, probably based on Church records or calculations, into his descriptions of the towns of New Spain. These data in Juan Díez de la Calle's description of the Indies, published in 1646,[25] make possible an estimate of Spanish population in New Spain about the middle of the seventeenth century.

Díez de la Calle gives data for ten of the towns and districts mentioned by López de Velasco. Fortunately these include the capital and towns in all major geographical areas of the colony. The estimates of both men are listed in table 5. Mexico City has been kept apart as a special instance which would distort any calculation of trend for the rest of the colony. The ratio between the two sets of data is 1.67. Applying this ratio to the total of Spanish vecinos for New Spain in 1570 exclusive of the capital, derived from López de

TABLE 5

NUMBERS OF SPANISH VECINOS IN TOWNS FOR WHICH DATA ARE AVAILABLE, 1570–1646

Town	1640 Díez de la Calle	Folio references in Díez de la Calle	1570 López de Velasco
Acapulco	150	60[r]	50
Puebla	1,000	61[r]	500
Tlaxcala	200	67[r]	50
Atlixco Valley[a]	1,000	67[v]	1,000
Veracruz	500	68[v]	200
Valladolid (Pátzcuaro for 1570)	250	71[v]	100
Oaxaca	600	78[v]–79[r]	350
Zacatecas	500	93[r]	300
Durango	120	94[v]–95[r]	30
Total	4,320		2,580
Mexico City	8,000	43[v]–44[r]	3,000

[a] Not a town, but a relatively compact area of settlement.

Velasco, (10,061 – 3,000) gives 11,792 for 1646. Adding to this the 8,000 vecinos stated by Díez de la Calle to be the Spanish population of Mexico City we get a total of 19,792 Spanish vecinos in New Spain proper or a lay white population of 118,752.

There still remain the clergy. According to Díez de la Calle, there were more than 6,000 clergy in all of the bishoprics suffragan to the archbishop of Mexico.[26] The dioceses of Yucatán, Chiapa, Guatemala, and Nicaragua were poor, with far fewer clergy than the central Mexico bishoprics, but the diocese of Guatemala was rich and had a relatively large number of clergy. The figure 2,000 would seem a reasonable deduction for all of these dioceses, hence, 4,000 is a reasonable estimate for secular clergy in the bishoprics of New Spain proper. For regular clergy, perhaps 3,000 would be a conservative estimate. The total for all clergy in New Spain proper *ca.* 1646 is 7,000.

However, some allowance must be made for the small numbers of Indians and mestizos who by that date had succeeded in entering upon careers in the Church; they may have numbered perhaps 500, a value which is a pure guess. The white clergy of New Spain, then, numbered perhaps 6,500. This figure added to the value for lay population gives an estimate of 125,252 for the white population of New Spain proper near the middle of the seventeenth century.

As a check upon this estimate, for 1646, the data in Díez de la Calle may be extended through comparison with the careful listing of district estimates prepared in 1774 by Pedro Alonso O'Crouley.[27] This count was probably based upon parish estimates forwarded to Mexico City and from there to Madrid. Table 6 lists towns for which both Díez de la Calle and O'Crouley furnish data. As before, Mexico City has been kept apart as a special instance. The table is not a good sample, since too many of the towns are in the north, where the population increased very rapidly in the eighteenth century, but it is the only source available at present. The ratio between the two sets of data is 0.144, which, applied to O'Crouley's estimate for all New Spain exclusive of the capital (79,314), gives a result of 11,421 Spanish vecinos. Combined with Díez de la Calle's estimate of 8,000 for Mexico City, this calculation gives 19,421 vecinos, or a lay white population of 115,526 for New Spain proper. This value is surprisingly close to the 118,752 derived by comparison of the data in Díez de la Calle and López de Velasco. With the allowance of 6,500 for white clergy, therefore, we may accept 125,000 as a tentative estimate for white population in New Spain proper near the middle of the seventeenth century.

To reduce the value of 125,000 to the area covered by the Cook and Simpson estimates of Indian numbers, we must still deduct an allowance for the white population in the areas beyond the limits of sedentary aboriginal population in the middle sixteenth century. Applying the ratio of 1.67 between the data in Díez de la Calle and those in López de Velasco to the value for the northern white population in 1570 gives a value of approximately 10,000. Since the northern population tended to increase at a more rapid rate than that in the central region, we may enlarge this figure slightly to 11,000. Our estimate for the Spanish population of central Mexico *ca.* 1646 accordingly is 114,000. This should be compared with the Cook and Simpson estimate of 1,500,000 for all elements and perhaps 1,200,000 for the Indians.

For the later seventeenth century, population data are still not available, although reports to the crown as yet uncovered in the Spanish archives probably contain estimates. During the eighteenth century the growth of popular interest in geography and statistics led to attempts to describe and estimate population in the Spanish dominions that provide exceptionally usable bases for calculation. In 1742, at the instance of the crown, Viceroy Conde de Fuenclara ordered that a general series of descriptions be pre-

TABLE 6

NUMBER OF SPANISH VECINOS IN TOWNS FOR WHICH DATA
ARE AVAILABLE, 1646–1774

Town	1774 O'Crouley	1646 Díez de la Calle
Acapulco	8	150
Puebla	13,000	1,000
Veracruz	1,300	500
Tlaxcala	400	200
Valladolid	2,500	250
San Luis Potosí	2,200	700[a]
Oaxaca	4,100	600
Zacatecas	2,800	500
Durango	3,500	120
San Bartolomé	300	40
Parral	300	250
Culiacán	80	80[b]
Total	30,488	4,390
Mexico City	50,000	8,000

[a] Juan Diez de la Calle, *op. cit.*, fol. 77ʳ.
[b] *Ibid.*, fols. 98ʳ–101ʳ.

pared for the parishes and towns of New Spain. These were excerpted by the then royal cosmographer, Antonio Villaseñor y Sánchez, into another of the useful compendia which form landmarks in the history of Spanish colonial administration in America.[28] Estimates for the total number of Spanish vecinos and other demographic elements in the bishoprics of New Spain were not included in the published work, perhaps because the Spanish crown did not wish to spread too exact an idea of the nature of its dominions among foreigners likely to be its enemies. However, the totals have been discovered in the Archivo General de la Nación, Mexico.[29] The figures for Spanish vecinos in the dioceses of New Spain proper are listed in table 7.

Multiplied by a factor of six for the social family, the estimates in table 7 give a total of 558,492 as the lay white population of New Spain proper. If 8,000 is accepted tentatively as a conservative allowance for the white clergy,[30] the number of white persons in New Spain in 1742 was 564,492, or in a rounded term to emphasize the fact that this is an estimate, 565,000.

To reduce the estimate of 565,000 for white population of New Spain proper in 1742 to a calculation for central Mexico requires subtracting

TABLE 7

NUMBERS OF SPANISH FAMILIES IN NEW SPAIN, ACCORDING
TO VILLASEÑOR Y SÁNCHEZ, 1746

Bishopric	Families
Mexico	55,662
Puebla	10,096
Michoacán	13,877
Oaxaca	2,305
Guadalajara	6,059
Durango	5,083
Total	93,082

the population of the bishopric of Durango, which embraced most of the northern mining area, and also deducting an allowance for the Bajío and adjacent basins. These rich agricultural lands were gaining very rapidly in population in the eighteenth century.[31] They were divided almost entirely between the dioceses of Michoacán and Guadalajara, but a small area in the northeast was assigned to the archbishopric of Mexico, which also had jurisdiction over mining and agricultural areas beyond the limits set here for central Mexico. A value of 100,000 for lay and ecclesiastical population in the north does not seem high, especially in view of the estimate arrived at below for population in 1772. The estimate for the white population in central Mexico in 1742, then, is 465,000.

A generation after the survey ordered by the Conde de Fuenclara, another general survey of New Spain was prepared by royal command in the years 1771–1774. Church statistics and estimates were again the basis for population data. In 1774 the calculations for white population were excerpted into a description of New Spain by a Hispanicized Irishman, Pedro Alonso O'Crouley. Since O'Crouley's work, which still remains in manuscript,[32] lists estimates for each town and district, it has been possible to separate his statistics for towns in the northern mining area and the Bajío from those for central Mexico. Table 8 gives the number of Spanish families in each bishopric with an additional breakdown into numbers in the northern and central regions. The lay white population of New Spain proper *ca.* 1772 was thus approximately 775,884, of whom 195,780 were in the north and 580,104 in the central regions of the colony. If we set the white ecclesiastical population at 8,000,[33] which is probably too low, and assign 2,000 to the north and 6,000 to the central regions, the number of

TABLE 8

NUMBERS OF SPANISH FAMILIES IN NEW SPAIN, ACCORDING TO O'CROULEY, 1774

Bishopric	New Spain proper	North	Central area
Mexico	59,980	3,215	56,765
Puebla	22,090	......	22,090
Michoacán	19,815	14,610	5,205
Oaxaca	4,619	......	4,619
Guadalajara	12,655	4,650	8,005
Durango	10,155	10,155	......
Total	129,314	32,630	96,684

white persons in New Spain proper *ca.* 1772 was approximately 784,000. Of this number, 198,000 lived beyond and 586,000 within the limits of sedentary Indian settlement as these had been more than two centuries earlier when the Spanish were first establishing themselves in Anáhuac.

Between 1790 and 1793 the viceregal government of New Spain undertook what came closest in the colonial period to a census in present-day terms. The results were tabulated in the viceregal secretariat and estimates prepared for the areas omitted in the enumeration: the Intendancies of Guadalajara and Veracruz and the province of Coahuila. The tabulation was copied by Alexander von Humboldt and reproduced in his celebrated *Essai politique sur le royaume de la Nouvelle-Espagne*. The tabulation gives a value for all elements in the colony in 1793 of 4,483,529.[34] Suggesting that this figure be increased by a sixth to allow for the widespread evasion of the count which occurred because the population feared that it would be used as the basis for tax levies, Humboldt indicated a value of 5,230,784 or in round numbers, 5,200,000 as the population of the colony in 1793.[35] Cook and Simpson accepted this figure but examined many of the census data independently. They arrived at 3,700,000 as a reasonable estimate for all elements in the population of central Mexico in 1793.[36] Cook (1942) further arrived at 20.1 per cent as the average ratio for white persons in the population of the central region exclusive of the capital.[37] His ratio is approximately midway between the 18.04 per cent suggested for the entire colony by Humboldt's contemporary, the *Contador-General* Fernando de Navarro y Noriega, who attempted an independent reworking of the census data,[38] and the 22.66 per cent suggested by Alexander von Humboldt.[39] Applying Cook's ratio to the population of the central region less the 125,000 Humboldt suggests as the population of the capital[40] ·(3,700,000 − 125,000 = 3,575,000) gives 718,575 as the white population of central Mexico exclusive of Mexico City.

The only data available for estimating the white population in the capital is Humboldt's reporting of the 1793 census. Like his estimates for the population of the colony, his statements on the number of whites in Mexico City show some discrepancies. In discussing the ratio of men to women, Humboldt lists 52,706 white persons in the capital but his figures for all elements in Mexico City total only 104,760[41] as against the census count of 112,926, which in turn must be increased by a sixth to allow for evasion. Fortunately, the discrepancy is small, and the ratio of whites to all elements is in fairly close agreement with Humboldt's statement elsewhere in the *Essai politique* that according to the 1793 census there were 51 white for every 100 inhabitants in the capital.[42] It seems probable, moreover, that almost no adjustment for evasion on the part of the whites is necessary, since they, as a more prominent element in the population, would have found it difficult to avoid being counted. Accordingly we may accept 60,000 as a reasonable allowance for the white population in the capital in 1793. The estimate for whites in central Mexico in 1793, then, is 778,575 or, in round numbers, 780,000.

To complete these estimates of white population, we shall calculate the number in New Spain proper in 1793. Humboldt gives 1,095,000 in a population of 4,832,100.[43] His total agrees neither with the summary prepared by the viceregal secretariat, nor with any of his revisions of the base figures.[44] However, on examination his estimate for whites does not seem excessive. If we deduct 45,000 for the intendancy of Yucatán, which had a very small Spanish population, we are left with 1,050,000 as the number of so-called white persons in New Spain proper. Of these, 270,000 would be the estimate for persons reckoned as Spaniards in the Bajío and regions farther north.

This value is in fair agreement with the estimated number of whites in the north in 1772 if we postulate a continued but somewhat less rapid increase in population during the two decades between 1772 and 1793. The slackening in the rate of increase in explained by the serious set-backs from famine and epidemic which the lower class population suffered in those decades.[45]

THE DISCREPANCY IN DEMOGRAPHIC TRENDS: THE LONG DEPRESSION OF THE MIDDLE COLONIAL PERIOD

Table 9 lists the estimates of white population arrived at here for New Spain proper and for the central region, the latter being defined as the

TABLE 9

So-Called White Population of New Spain in the Colonial Period

Year	New Spain proper	Central Mexico
1570	63,000	57,000
1646	125,000	114,000
1742	565,000	465,000
1772	784,000	586,000
1793	1,050,000	780,000

region between the Isthmus of Tehuantepec and the northernmost limit of sedentary Indian settlement in the middle sixteenth century. The values should be compared with the Cook and Simpson estimates of Indian population for the sixteenth and seventeenth centuries listed in table 1.

From these figures, it is clear that the white and near-white European group in the population and the Indian majority showed widely differing demographic trends. If we ignore the period 1519–1550 which witnessed the demographic destruction attendant upon the Conquest and the first generation of European settlement, when the white element was taking root, the divergence was sharpest in the period from the great matlazahuatl epidemic of 1576–1579 to the end of the seventeenth century, more than a hundred years. During this period the white group steadily increased at the same time that the Indian first suffered a sharp drop, then moved further downward at a decelerating rate to the bottom of the curve, and began a slow recovery.

The significance of this difference in trends lies in the fact that the white and near-white population of the Spanish cities lived on Indian tributes and services. Manual labor and even many of the skilled crafts were held to be beneath the dignity of Europeans so that for the service provided by the relatively small number of white artisans and Negro slaves, the white townsfolk ate food raised by Indians, clothed themselves in materials produced by Indians and in most instances worked into cloth by them, lived in houses built by Indians and largely furnished by them, and remitted to Europe specie mined and processed largely by Indians.[46]

Moreover, the great number of Indian workmen available during the period 1521–1576 accustomed the white population to lavish use of labor. Spanish households literally teemed with Indian servants, even the poorest whites being entitled to relief from domestic tasks.[47] Vast construction projects, both civil and religious, were carried out by hand methods in surprisingly short periods of time. Motolinía has given us a striking description of the hordes of workmen who were used to build the new Spanish capital after the destruction of Tenochtitlán; because of the great number of deaths among the workers, he regarded the construction as one of the major plagues decimating the Indians.

The seventh plague was the building of the great city of Mexico, for during the early years more people were employed in that than in building the temple of Jerusalem at the time of Solomon. So many people were working on the buildings, or carried materials, or brought tributes and supplies for the Spaniards and the workmen, that a man could scarcely make his way through some of the streets and along some of the causeways, wide though these are. Many [workmen] were killed by [falling] beams; others fell from upper stories; others were killed by the caving in of buildings they were wrecking. The custom was that the Indians paid all the costs themselves, finding materials themselves, and paying the stone-cutters, masons, and carpenters; and if they did not bring their own food, they fasted. They carried all materials on their backs [except for] the beams and large stones which they dragged with ropes. Since they lacked skill and had plenty of workmen, when they needed a hundred men to handle a stone or beam, four hundred brought it. It is an Indian custom that while they are carrying materials, they being many, they go along singing and shouting. The sound of their singing and shouting hardly died down night and day because of the great energy that went into the building of the city during the first years.[48] ·

This description can hardly be counted an exaggeration. When Hernán Cortés completed the façade galleries on one side of his palace in Mexico City, *ca.* 1531–1532, the Indians of Coyoacán, according to their later claims for payment, furnished hundreds of workmen in addition to ordinary allotments. The Indians supplied 320 men for four days to bring to the city the eight stone bases for the columns; 640 men for six days to bring the stone columns; 320 men for six days to bring the corbels; 400 men for a day to bring 400 white stones for the staircase; 1,200 men for two days to bring wooden beams; 600 men for two days to bring lime; 160 men for three days to bring up and put in place the wooden grillwork. Moreover, the town of Coyoacán had to prepare and furnish the planks to roof the building, the windows and doorways, and the grillwork.[49]

After the first surge of construction of the capital, the clergy proceeded to use far greater numbers of workmen to dot central Mexico with imposing churches and convents. The regular clergy were perhaps the greatest users of construction labor in New Spain during the sixteenth century. One of their larger projects, the great fortress convent and church of Yanhuitlán, has walls of dressed stone, the thickness of which must be measured in meters. It was built in twenty-five years, almost entirely by hand labor, even to the carrying of stones and other materials. A medieval European city of the same size as Yanhuitlán but making far greater use of animal traction power, would have required centuries to construct a comparable cathedral church. Far from being an isolated instance, Yanhuitlán was typical of religious architecture in many other Indian communities such as Teposcolula, Coixtlahuaca, Tepeaca, Cholula, Huejotzingo, and Yuririapúndaro, to name but a few.[50] The enormous reservoir of labor the Spaniards found in their new colony made possible building at a speed and on a scale equaled few times in the history of mankind before the Industrial Revolution.

With the sharp drop in the Indian population during the epidemic of 1576–1579, the Europeans were faced with a substantial decrease in the number of people available for labor of all kinds. Thereafter, they were faced with further steady shrinkage in Indian numbers at the same time that the number of Europeans steadily rose and with it the demand for more labor to provide services at the accustomed high level of consumption.

The Spanish problem was complicated by the fact that Negro slaves, an alternative form of labor imported for the most part directly from Africa, proved to possess none of the Europeans' immunity to disease, but died in the epidemics as readily as the Indians.[51] As a result, the viceregal administrations found themselves beset by urgent appeals for allotments of Indian laborers from former slave owners. On May 10, 1586, for example, Viceroy

Marqués de Villamanrrique reported to the crown that virtually all of the slaves employed in the mines had died in the great epidemic of 1576–1579, and the miners, in consequence, were faced with ruin unless they were permitted to use forced Indian labor. Despite express royal instructions to the contrary, the previous viceroy and Villamamrrique himself had been forced to acquiesce in circumvention of the royal orders.[52] The following year, Jerónimo López, an official of the Audiencia of Mexico, petitioned for and received an allotment of Indians to be used as sheepherders to replace dead Negro slaves.[53] His petition was but one of many. However unwilling the viceregal administrators, additional Indians had to be allocated from the shrinking labor reservoir to replace workmen for many enterprises that previously had relied upon Negroes.[54]

We may distinguish a number of factors which after 1576 determined the success or failure of the European upper stratum in satisfying its labor demand. Three have already been indicated as especially important: decline in the total number of workmen available, rise in the number of Europeans, and the lavish use of labor. A fourth factor, efficiency of production, may be passed over on the ground that it was probably nearly constant except for the few changes which will be discussed later. As has already been mentioned, there may have been a slightly improved rate of yield in Indian agriculture because the shrinking population would tend to concentrate its efforts on the best of its land and retire marginal land from use. Furthermore, the adoption of European agricultural techniques, crops, and livestock tended to increase efficiency of production. But the improvements in yield must have been virtually insignificant relative to the effect of the disappearance of a large proportion of the cultivators. In mining, wider adoption of the patio process based upon quicksilver, use of gunpowder for blasting, and the development of the animal-powered whim (*malacate*) for drainage made for somewhat increased efficiency, but again, although the use of gunpowder and the malacate were known at least by the beginning of the seventeenth century, really widespread application of these did not begin until the end of that century.

A fifth factor, efficiency of the methods developed for procuring labor from the Indian towns, became especially important after 1576. In the circumstances obtaining after that date, a progressively larger percentage of adult Indians had to be procured for service. Failure to do so would mean that the Europeans would be unable to maintain their previous level of labor use and would enter into a period of curtailment. If the degree of failure should be large, curtailment might well become stringency and economic distress.

The evidence available, although fragmentary, points to the appearance of precisely such stringency and even distress after 1575. The data are perhaps most striking in the matter of the procurement of food and fuel for the Spanish cities. During the early and middle decades of the sixteenth century, the Spanish population was amply supplied with food, firewood, and fodder. The bulk of these supplies, that is, maize, vegetables, fruit, fish, game, firewood, grass, and hay, were supplied directly by the Indians either as tribute in kind or as produce brought to the Spanish cities for sale. Wheat and livestock were supplied largely from Spanish-owned farms.[55] The decrease in Indian population meant an almost automatic corresponding decrease in supplies derived as tribute and apparently also in those brought to the cities for sale. Furthermore, the drop in labor supply made it difficult for Spanish farmers to raise the same quantity of wheat and livestock as before, let alone meet a growing demand. As a result, the Spanish cities were confronted with a decrease in supplies and even a serious shortage for the first time since they were founded. This new stringency gave rise to continuing complaints and anxious reports by the viceroys to the crown.

Two statements by the younger Velasco (1589–1595, 1607–1611) may be taken as unusually eloquent but otherwise typical descriptions of the plight of the Spanish element in the colony. On April 6, 1595, Velasco wrote to Philip II:

I have reported to Your Majesty on other occasions concerning the need and general shortage which this land is suffering and which is increasing daily because of the many who come from abroad and the natural increase among those here, for they have no way to earn a living. It is true that many are citizens of cities (aside from traders, of whom few are wealthy) but all others in general are in want. I am concerned, for among them are honest and worthy men whom it would be wise to have grateful and contented against occasions and events that time might bring. There are no positions as justices for the fourth part of those who claim recompense for their services or the services of their forebears, nor can any form of maintenance be provided from the revenues from vacant posts, or through granting monopolies of wine or meat, or in any other manner as there used to be in the time of my predecessors, for I abolished all such monopolies on the ground that they were contrary to conscience. [As a result] many are complaining, while I am dumb and confused, and even unpopular and hateful, because I cannot give aid to some to supply their needs. Since the people here are used to excessive freedom, they talk at length, and, in order to avoid worse difficulties, I must bear their murmuring as long as they do not become insolent in public.

Until now much of the need of these people was met by the abundance of foodstuffs and other supplies. However, since those who consume are many and the Indians who produce are few, supplies have become so short that this year no one has come forward to contract to supply meat, for neither sheep nor cattle are to be found. All supplies are becoming scarce and are rising in price so fast that before many years this land will experience as great a dearth and want as now exists in Spain...[56]

A few months after writing this letter, Velasco repeated his warnings in his advice to the Count of Monterrey, his successor.

The abundance of turkeys and chickens in this kingdom has vanished, and what there are are sold at excessive prices. This evil is due to regrating and to the idleness and negligence of the Indians... I have seen the supply [of meat] decrease so greatly that although I once knew a time when the term Indies implied meat in plenty and at moderate price, all that is now ended. There is no supply of meat, nor can needed amounts be obtained even at the high price meat now commands. Although I have taken far-reaching measures, have issued new ordinances, regulated [livestock] branding, have appointed inspectors and have forbidden under heavy penalty the slaughter of cows and other female livestock, I do not see that I have been able to repair the damage or restore the herds of livestock to their former great numbers. The worst of it is that I do not know what other measure might be applied that might work...

Especially notable is the harm which comes from the Indians' failure to raise crops, for in addition to the rising cost of foodstuffs, the lack of them [even at high prices] will be the ruin and destruction of this land.... Forcing the Indians to sow and cultivate their lands (which are abundant and fertile) is a matter of the greatest importance for this realm and one which should be given special attention in the future....[57]

The measures adopted by the viceregal and municipal administrations are further testimony to the existence of continuing and serious shortages of foodstuffs and other supplies. In November, 1578, two years after the outbreak of the epidemic of 1576, Viceroy Enríquez ordered the establishment of a state granary (*alhóndiga*) in Mexico City which was to buy grain and sell it to consumers at fixed prices whenever supplies became short or prices rose too high. Although begun as a temporary expedient, the alhóndiga soon became permanent.[58] Other Spanish cities quickly established similar granaries, to which residents or near-by farmers were ordered to bring supplies of grain. In 1579 the alhóndiga system was supplemented by a crude system of allocation imposed upon *encomenderos* receiving maize as tribute: those within fourteen leagues of the capital were ordered to sell a third of their maize to the Mexico City alhóndiga, the royal treasury being held to this requirement like any other receiver of tribute. The grain was to be sold at the price of 1576, until then the highest that had been paid for royal tribute maize at public auction, but considerably less than maize had been bringing in private sale. Outside of the radius of fourteen leagues, the encomenderos were to hold a third of their tribute maize for sale at the viceroy's orders. This last provision was inserted to provide a supply for the mines and other Spanish settlements that might be in need.[59] The two series of measures established what was in effect a sixteenth-century attempt at rationing.

A third series of ordinances attempted to handle the problem of rising prices and short supplies by the only other devices known to sixteenth- and seventeenth-century legislators: price-fixing, prohibition of regrating or any form of purchase for resale, and assigning set market areas for trade. In June, 1578, the Audiencia of Mexico adopted an ordinance setting prices for maize, for, ran the text, the price had been "rising in such manner ... that not even those who have wealth and businesses can bear the cost ..."[60]

Four months later, in October, 1578, the ordinance was repealed on the ground that harvests were good and prices low.[61] This was the last time in more than a century that an ordinance regulating sale or distribution of foodstuffs was repealed. The very next month, November, 1578, a new and more stringent ordinance was promulgated to forbid hoarding or purchase for resale of wheat, oats, and barley; according to this new ordinance, maize was again scarce.[62] In the following years, the prohibitions against buying for resale or hoarding were extended to virtually all forms of foodstuffs, fodder, and firewood. In 1583 residents of the capital were forbidden to go outside the city, along the causeways, canals, or roads, to buy supplies from Indians bringing them to market. For people of low degree, presumably not white, and for mixed-bloods, the penalty for violation was set at 100 lashes in addition to the fine to be levied against all offenders. In 1619 the punishment for *personas viles* was raised to the frightful penalty of 200 lashes and two years in the galleys. Trading in foodstuffs and other supplies in the capital finally was ordered limited to public squares, legally designated market places, and the state storehouse, definite places and days being assigned for the sale of each commodity. Even in the state alhóndigas, sales were ordered to be made by direct trading, no third parties being permitted to intervene. These regulations were enacted for the most part not merely once but repeatedly in the half-century after 1579 for which information is available.[63] Similar ordinances were enacted in other Spanish settlements. However much the effectiveness of this legislation in alleviating the shortages may be questioned, all of it testifies to the existence of severe economic strain.

Unfortunately, quantitative data, which alone could give a relatively precise idea of the movement of production for the cities, are almost completely lacking. In 1632 the wheat farmers of Tacuba complained to Viceroy Marqués de Cerralvo, that according to tithe records their farms had once grown 6,000 *fanegas* of wheat a year but by 1631 their yield had decreased to 1,090 fanegas.[64] For the same years at least some decrease in yield occurred also in the valley of Atlixco, the capital's chief source of supply, for in 1632 the Marqués de Cerralvo commented that, although the valley had once grown more than 150,000 fanegas of wheat a year, it no longer did so.[65] These may have been extreme instances. They occurred at a time when the great drainage works for the valley of Mexico were drawing off a large number of the remaining Indian laborers; but they indicate that in 1631–1632 the capital with its increasing population was faced not merely with stationary but decreasing food supplies and actual famine.

The meager tithe data available also support the hypothesis that the Spanish cities were having difficulty in securing foodstuffs. Tithes are especially significant data because they were levied upon Spanish agriculture and stockraising, upon tributes paid to Spaniards, upon Old World crops and livestock raised by Indians, and upon community enterprises conducted by Indian villages to secure cash for tributes and community expenses. They thus represent a rough index to the amount of foodstuffs brought to the cities for sale. In New Galicia and Durango, yields declined in terms of money during the first quarter of the seventeenth century, although the decline was moderate.[66] In Oaxaca during the same period, tithe yields remained approximately stationary in money terms.[67] Since prices were rising, even a stationary yield meant decline in real production, and a small decrease in money yield meant a far sharper decline in terms of quantities of food raised. Again, these data are meager and deal with peripheral areas, but they too suggest that the Spanish cities were receiving smaller quantities of supplies to feed their growing populations.

All of the data available point to the conclusion that only in the best years after 1576–1579 through much of the seventeenth century were the white inhabitants able to secure easily sufficient food to feed themselves and the servants and workmen directly dependent upon them. Factors other than the labor supply were probably operative in this period; the unexplained drop in numbers of livestock at the end of the sixteenth and in the early decades of the seventeenth century can hardly have been due to lack of herdsmen alone;[68] but labor supply was probably the most important factor present in a continuing shortage of foodstuffs and other items of urban supply. For the first generation after 1576 the decrease in supplies may have meant only the disappearance of previous abundance, not actual hunger except in years of crop failure, whereas before 1576 even in years of crop failure the white element had plentiful supplies. After 1595 the failure of production to keep pace with a still rising white population may well have meant for the first time since the Conquest of New Spain that the white element faced a deficit in foodstuffs sufficient to place its lower groups chronically on the verge of hunger. In poor crop years such as those of 1623–1625, and during the construction of the great drainage works for Mexico City, the Spanish urban population lived in a state of fright because of the threat of famine and the supposed danger of uprising by the starving Indians.

In mining, the evidence also points unmistakably to a severe and continuing shortage of labor directly owing to the shrinkage in Indian population. The mines of Pachuca will serve as an illustration. Before the great epidemic of 1576–1579 these mines drew 1,108 Indians a week through a draft on the surrounding villages. On September 23, 1580, because of the depopulation of these villages, the draft was adjusted to provide only 711 workmen at a time.[69] By 1607 they were supplying only 350 workmen. An investigation in that year, initiated with the intention of drawing out more labor, led to a new assessment providing for no more than 300.[70] By 1661 the villages, which before 1576–1579 were furnishing 1,108 workmen, supplied only 19. A new investigation and a new assessment in 1661 which brought additional villages into the operation of the labor draft could provide a steady force of only 57 Indians a week.[71] A drop as severe as that at Pachuca was perhaps an extreme instance, but the other mining districts faced a sufficiently critical shrinkage in their available labor supply to lead viceroys to search frantically for labor for the colony's key industry.[72]

If the most important fields of economic activity, food production and mining, were critically short of labor throughout most of the century after 1576–1579, the conclusion is unavoidable that other fields less favored with viceregal aid must have been experiencing at least the same and probably an even more severe dearth of labor.[73]

In addition to the diminution in labor and food supplies, brought about by the drop in Indian population, further hardships fell on the Spanish in the form of decreases in tributes, tithes, and fees of administration, all of which responded rapidly to demographic change. Tributes were reassessed relatively frequently in order to bring them into relation with the actual number of Indian adults; tithes responded directly to changes in production; and fees of administration tended to vary with the number of people in the districts. Rises in money wages and prices[74] consequent upon shortages of labor and supplies must have compounded the initial effects and extended them to other sectors of the economy. In addition to difficulty in procuring labor, the miners, who received a fixed price for their principal product, silver, found themselves caught between rising costs and heavy state taxation, which left at best a precarious and slender margin of profit.[75] The general rise in prices was also keenly felt by large sections of the Spanish population: encomenderos, who derived their incomes directly from tributes; members of the Church hierarchy and crown bureaucracies, who received tithes, fees, and salaries; and the state pensioners, who lived on small treasury grants. These groups were dependent on fixed or shrinking sources of income. The plight of the salaried Spaniards is illustrated by the plea of the *oidores* of the royal audiencia for an increase in wages, which was transmitted by Viceroy Velasco II in 1590 to the notoriously unsympathetic Philip II, who was preoccupied with his own fiscal difficulties.

Some time ago the oidores of this royal audiencia petitioned Your Majesty for an increase in salary because of the growing dearness of foodstuffs and other supplies needed for living in this land. In addition to the general rise in prices, houses and rents have become especially dear because of the large number of people, so that any decent house now rents for four hundred pesos a year, that is nearly a fifth of an oidor's salary. Since Your Majesty has commanded that no oidor may own his own house, [the audiencia] again petitions [for an increase in salary.] It is indeed true that this land is very dear [to live in] and that houses command exhorbitant rents...[76]

A large number of white families must have found themselves reduced from comparative wealth to straitened circumstances as the drop in the Indian population forced a downward spiral in the economy of the European stratum.

The beginning of the downward spiral clearly must be placed in the great epidemic of 1576–1579. The end of the period of shortage is much less easy to establish with our present scanty information about the seventeenth century in Mexico. It must have been a gradual improvement, occurring at varying rates in the different fields of economic activity, with no spectacular general upswing to fix a sharp, easily discernible end. On the basis of population recovery, the terminal limit would probably be the last decades of the seventeenth century, although in the 1690's there may have been a sharp resumption of pressure when a prolonged series of crop failures plunged the colony into near-famine conditions paralleling those of the 1620's. The economic depression besetting the Spanish cities because of the shrinkage of the Indian base lasted more than a century.

The degree of distress during this long period is also difficult to assess. The century or more of depression probably did not mean continuously acute misery except for the Indians, who seemed doomed to relentless extinction. For the Spanish cities, it meant at the least the economic constriction which would follow a decrease in the supplies and services available per capita. When bad crop years or need for great expenditure of labor brought further adverse factors, the cities undoubtedly had intervals of actual crisis. At other times such as a rare year of unusually good crops, they may have had temporary respite from some of the pressure. In spite of contractions in the supply of production and services after 1576, there was, in general, a sufficient margin for a steady, if slow, growth in Spanish population from 1570 to 1646 and a more rapid increase in the decades following. Living conditions in New Spain were probably better than those obtaining among similar populations in the Iberian Peninsula and the rest of Europe. However, the economy could no longer provide the opulence of the early and middle decades of sixteenth-century New Spain, and the Spanish, whatever their resentment and resistance, were forced to surrender much of their earlier well-being.

The passage of the Spanish cities through this century of depression may go far to explain many of the phenomena and changes of the so-called dark century. In economic and demographic terms, it may indeed have been dark. The long depression certainly accelerated many social and economic changes, some of which will be discussed below. Shrinkage in the margin available for the support of a white leisure class may explain in part the relative cultural impoverishment of the early and middle decades of the seventeenth century as compared with the brilliance of the sixteenth and eighteenth centuries.

ECONOMIC DIFFICULTIES ELSEWHERE IN THE SPANISH EMPIRE

The economic difficulties besetting the cities of New Spain were hardly unique in the Spanish empire. They were almost certainly paralleled by similar developments in the major Spanish colonies in the New World, for Guatemala, the Audiencia of Quito, Upper and Lower Peru, New Granada, and Tierra Firme[77] suffered similar catastrophic reductions in the numbers of natives. The decrease in the laboring and tribute-paying strata in those colonies almost certainly entailed many, if not all, of the same consequences as in New Spain.

During the same period the imperial center also developed serious weakness, for after 1575 Spain herself entered upon an economic and demographic decline that was not arrested until the beginning of the eighteenth century.[78] The mother country's loss of economic strength meant additional difficulty for her colonies. The inability of Spain to absorb colonial exports of wool, hides, dyes, and other products may well have contributed to a falling off in production of these commodities in New Spain. Similarly, the growing inability of Spanish industries to provide manufactures for the Spanish cities of the colony in needed quantities and at relatively low prices aggravated the difficulties arising from deficits in colonial production.[79] Fewer economic opportunities and a worsening of living conditions in Spain also meant that numbers of Spaniards migrated to the colony, where, bad though economic conditions may have been, food was still more abundant throughout the late sixteenth century and most of the seventeenth century than in Spain. Because of the nature of colonial society, these immigrants meant little if any addition to the labor force in New Spain, but rather an increase in the number of people to be fed.[80] Finally, the fiscal straits of the Spanish crown forced it to press for more funds from the colony. Accordingly it imposed additional taxes; sold almost all offices; sought payments for grants, favors, and pardons of almost all description; and pleaded for loans and gifts,[81] all of which represented a further burden placed on the Spanish cities. At the same time, the weakened economy of the colony was far less able to succor the hard-pressed Spanish crown in its needs. Through their coincidence in time, the economic and demographic crises of Spain and her colony thus interacted to the disadvantage of both.

SOLUTIONS TO PROBLEMS OF FOOD SUPPLY AND LABOR:
THE HACIENDA, THE REPARTIMIENTO,
DEBT PEONAGE

The Spanish towns of New Spain not only survived this long period of economic contraction but unlike the mother country also gained strength during it as is evident from their steady, if slow increase in population from 1570 to 1646 and their rapid increase in the century following. Their survival, and even quasi-prosperity, resulted not from grim endurance but rather from the success of at least some of the measures they took to meet the major problems of service and production.

An obvious measure was to reduce the lavish consumption of labor. The mere difficulty of finding workers would bring about a decrease in the number of servants in Spanish households and in much labor used for less necessary purposes. The vast construction projects characteristic of the earlier sixteenth century were curtailed almost automatically after 1576–1579. According to George Kubler, the number of building projects which the religious orders had under construction reached a peak in the decades of the 1570's, probably before the outbreak of the epidemic in 1576. It fell off sharply in the 1580's and again in the 1590's, rising slightly in the decade 1601–1610 before falling again in the decade 1611–1620 to the lowest level in ninety years. Since the building of the great monastic churches and convents had absorbed much of the available Indian labor, this curtailment in construction meant a distinct drop in the demands on the Indian population. Kubler suggests that the reduction resulted from the realization of the religious orders that enough churches had been built to care for the population, particularly the much smaller population in existence after 1579.[82] Some of the viceregal orders indicate that the reduction was also brought about by decision of the royal government that labor could not be found in sufficient amount to provide for the needs of the Spanish as well as for the greater glory of God.[83]

This curtailment of construction extended to building by the secular clergy. The main structure of the cathedral of Mexico, begun in its present form in 1573, required approximately a century to build, against the short periods in which equally substantial edifices were completed in earlier decades.[84] Lay building, both private and official, must also have been sharply reduced to judge by the cessation of the construction of the great colonial palaces in Mexico City in the century 1576–1675. The one major exception was, of course, the works for drainage of the valley of Mexico.

Curtailment in building construction and in other uses of labor must have meant substantial economy in labor demand compared with the decades 1541–1570. However, the shortage of food and labor for the mines during the very period when this curtailment was taking place indicates clearly that mere curtailment was not the solution.

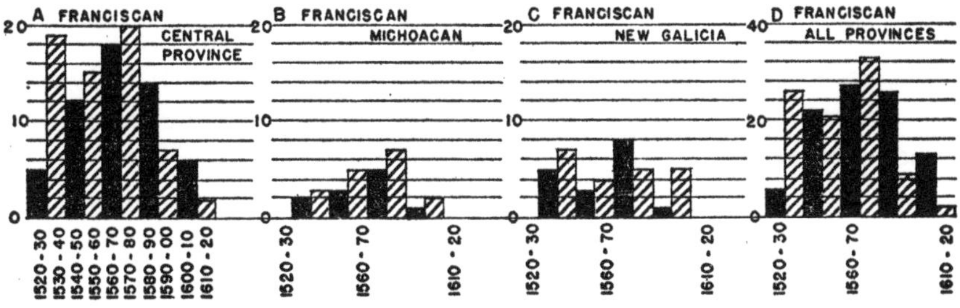

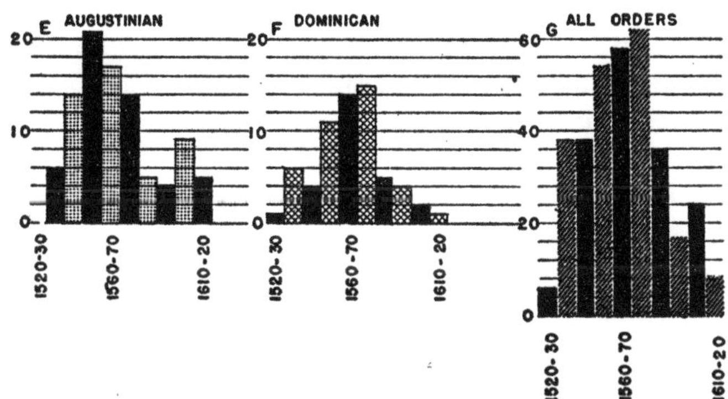

Fig. 1. Amount of building by the religious orders in New Spain, 1520–1620. Source: George Kubler, *Mexican Architecture of the Sixteenth Century* (New Haven, Yale University Press, 1948). Reproduced by courtesy of the Yale University Press.

Other measures to solve the problem reorganized the basis of food production and the means of securing labor. The earliest and most acutely felt manifestation of the impact upon the Spanish cities of the decrease in the Indian population was scarcity and even lack of food. As has already been pointed out, before 1576–1579 the Spanish population, particularly in the central and southern parts of Mexico, relied directly on the Indian communities for virtually all foodstuffs, fuel, and fodder; the only significant exceptions being wheat and livestock. As supplies from the Indian communities steadily fell off, efforts were made to increase their food contribution by requiring them to pay a larger share of tributes in kind and by requiring each tributary to raise a number of chickens and turkeys and sell them at low fixed prices. A series of directives also ordered the *corregidores* and *alcaldes mayores* to see that the Indians raised as much foodstuff as possible. None of these measures seems to have had marked success perhaps because of difficulty in administration and because of passive Indian resistance to the imposition of any new burdens.[85] Moreover, commented Viceroy Velasco II, since the justices charged with enforcing the directives were not to receive any fees or other payment for their work, "I suspect that no one obeys the ordinance through the remissness of the justices, . . . who never direct any effort toward enforcing it."[86]

The solution to the problem of Spanish food supply lay in decreasing or eliminating direct dependence upon the enfeebled Indian communities. The most obvious solution was to extend to other essential crops the system of Spanish-owned large estates which were already raising wheat and livestock for the cities. Such estates were still dependent upon the Indian communities for labor, but the Indian population could be harnessed to food production much more efficiently in commercial agriculture as laborers working upon Spanish estates under Spanish supervision.

The rapid diffusion of Spanish latifundia which took place involved operation of complex factors about which we still know very little. In the northern mining area beyond the zone of pre-Conquest sedentary settlement, Spanish farms developed on the nearest arable land with sufficient water shortly after the opening of any new mine. The difficulty and excessive cost of moving food long distances by cart or pack train to feed the mining population made this development almost automatic. In the central and southern areas of Mexico this development need not have taken place so rapidly or to the extent that it did had the large sedentary Indian population furnished food in the desired amounts. It is true that powerful factors—the economic security of landownership, European example, the prestige attached to holding an estate, and the limited number of fields of economic activity open to an upper class in the sixteenth and seventeenth centuries—would have led the wealthier Spanish to acquire land in any event.[87] But had the demographic history of the colony been otherwise, had Spanish estates been forced to compete with a cheap, abundant, Indian-produced food supply, their growth would have been severely retarded and probably severely limited. As events turned out, the drop in Indian production gave Spanish-owned estates clear entry into the large and expanding market of the Spanish cities. Furthermore, the shrinkage in

Indian population made vacant vast areas of good agricultural land in the center and south, the so-called *tierras baldías*. These were legally crown lands which could be acquired only by royal or viceregal grant. Many Spaniards did indeed petition for and receive grants of such lands;[88] others simply took possession of likely tracts without formal title, to extend existing estates or to establish new ones.

Spanish occupation of tierras baldías implying the formation of latifundia took place rapidly in the 1570's, 1580's, and subsequent decades. The records of land grants for the Audiencia of Mexico show a steady increase in the areas allotted to private petitioners and in the size of the grants made.[89] By 1591 the crown, scenting an untapped source of revenue, ordered that thenceforth all grants be paid for rather than allotted as free gifts of the crown. After 1593 land grants had to be bought, and the revenue from them became a substantial item in the royal revenues—a further indication that sizable tracts were involved. The crown order of 1591 also complained that large areas were being occupied by Spaniards who neither secured grants from the crown nor made payments and ordered that such holdings be investigated and the occupants forced to pay for proper titles. The first *composiciones,* or settlements under which the crown issued clear title for payment, seem to have taken place in New Spain early in the seventeenth century. At first the composiciones to clear title were probably special arrangements by individual landholders. By the middle decades of the century it became customary for the crown to proclaim *composiciones generales,* periods of grace when any landholder might come forward to clear his titles on favorable terms of payment.[90] In addition to royal grants and private seizure of tierras baldías, the Spanish also acquired large tracts of land by purchase and rental from Indian holders.[91] Any large Spanish estate probably derived part of its lands by each of these methods in a continuing process of acquisition and occupation.

By the early 1590's the formation of Spanish-owned estates apparently reached a point at which, provided they could secure enough labor, their production could meet the food requirements of the Spanish cities.[92] This is not to say that the cities were freed from all reliance upon Indian production, but rather that in a pinch they could squeeze through upon food produced by the farms owned and controlled directly by their own vecinos. By 1603 the city of Guadalajara, for instance, was fed almost entirely from Spanish farms at Tlajomulco and the valley of Tlala.[93] Both areas are unusually large and relatively flat land surfaces peculiarly suited to plowing and hence European agriculture. Both could draw upon large reservoirs of labor, Tlajomulco being one of the most densely populated Indian areas near Guadalajara[94] and the valley of Tlala being adjacent to the province of Avalos, where the Indian population suffered least decline during the earlier colonial period.[95] In bad crop years Mexico City, the principal center of white population, was fed from Spanish farms in the valley of Atlixco,[96] again an unusually broad expanse of fertile soil well-suited to plowing and near large Indian towns which furnished labor. With the continuing development of Spanish-owned latifundia throughout the seventeenth century, the supply problem of the cities was probably made progressively easier. The worst of the long series of food shortages after 1576–1579 may have been over by the 1650's or 1660's,[97] although at best seventeenth- and eighteenth-century methods of agriculture on the high Mexican plateau never yielded a sufficient surplus to carry the colony through bad crop years without hunger.[98]

This development of large estates still left unsolved the basic problem of getting sufficient labor. Since the white and mestizo population could not easily be forced to provide manual labor, the only practicable alternative to the use of Indians was importation of Negro slaves from Africa. To a royal bureaucracy which was trying desperately to curtail the use of Indians to the number it could provide for fields, mines, and public works, the importation of Negroes appealed from the beginning as a long-term solution to the labor shortage. It was urged particularly for mining, which was chronically short of labor,[99] for enterprises which were regarded as of lesser usefulness to the community, such as sugar growing; and those which were regarded as being unusually dangerous to the Indians, such as sugar refineries (*ingenios*) and cloth mills (*obrages*). These last two were forbidden to employ Indians at all.[100] Use of Negroes also had the advantage of providing a more stable labor force than could a shifting Indian levy. This advantage and the efforts of crown officials led to a considerable use of Negroes; New Spain imported relatively large numbers of them during the later sixteenth and most of the seventeenth century.[101] However, the number of Negro slaves available was far too small for the needs of the Spanish, and purchase of Negroes required the investment of substantial sums which were lost if the Negroes died from overwork and disease, as many did within a short time. The Indians, on a wage basis of some kind, always remained the best available source of cheap labor in quantity. Even in sugar growing and milling and cloth weaving, the continuing cheapness of Indian labor led owners in the majority of enterprises to evade the viceregal prohibitions.[102] Crown-favored industries were even more insistent that their needs be met somehow from the cheaper and more abundant Indian labor.

The efforts of crown officials in New Spain to find labor for the important activities, such as food production, mining, and public works, which were held to be entitled to a state-enforced supply of Indians, led first to the development of an interesting system of labor levy. In the early and middle decades of the sixteenth century, the Indian towns were held to provide laborers under a fairly casual system of levy, either by the viceroy or local officials. Under the impact of the sharp reduction in population during 1576–1579 and subsequent years, Viceroys Enríquez and Villamanrrique elaborated this earlier levy into the rigid labor draft which has been called the *repartimiento, rueda,* or *tanda* system, the first name meaning allotment and the second two referring to the periodic turns of service.[103] Under this system Indian towns were forced to provide laborers on the basis of the frequent counts of population for tribute purposes. The quota was set at 4 per cent weekly of the tributaries in ordinary seasons and 10 per cent at the two peak agricultural seasons of *escarda* (crop thinning and weeding) and harvest.[104] The levy fell upon all Indian males more than fifteen and less than sixty years of age, except nobles and public officials. Married men were held to three weeks of service a year; unmarried adolescents were held to an extra week's turn of service ostensibly to keep them out of mischief.[105] Each week the allotted number of workers had to present themselves at a central point in each area so that a Spanish official called the *juez repartidor* (commissioner for allocation) could assign them to local employers for a week's work at a set wage. The laborers could be used only for specified activities and had to be used by the employer to whom they were allotted. By the time of Villamanrrique even to obtain a new allotment required a special order of the viceroy himself.[106] After 1580, in fact, New Spain was rationing Indian labor.

The effectiveness of the repartimiento in providing labor may be assessed in terms of the percentage of annual working time of Indian males held to labor that it secured for the Spanish. If we estimate unmarried adolescents fifteen and older to have been one-sixth of the total number of such males, the standard instruction to the *jueces repartidores* for mines called for approximately 6.08 per cent of total annual working time. This percentage does not count time spent in traveling to and from work, which for Indians sent to the mines may have meant from one to three more weeks a year lost to them although not gained by the Spanish. The rate of levy established for agriculture would have yielded approximately 6.3 per cent of the annual working time of Indian males held to labor, again with no allowance for time spent in going to and from work. The two figures are in sufficient agreement to suggest that the levy for mining was adjusted to give a proportion approximately the same as the levy for Spanish farmers.

Even at the higher value of 6.3 per cent, the repartimiento still gave a small yield indeed. By the second decade of the seventeenth century, when the quota for towns furnishing labor to agriculture (but not to the mines) was reduced to 2 per cent in ordinary periods although retained at 10 per cent for the two peak seasons,[107] the proportion of adult male Indian labor time secured for Spanish farms was lowered correspondingly to approximately 5.08 per cent of the Indian laborers' annual time. The continuing testimony of the viceroys reporting to the Spanish crown, the sharp competition for labor among Spanish employers, and the steady downward reassessments of laborers to be furnished by towns under the frequent tribute counts, all point unmistakably to the fact that as early as the first administration of Viceroy Velasco II (1590–1595) the repartimiento was failing to draft enough labor from the steadily declining Indian population to meet even those demands which the crown official recognized as having a clear prior claim on whatever workmen were available. Each reassessment meant a reduction of the allotments of workers to meet the new, lowered number of workmen the town could be held to provide.[108] It was this tightness of labor which led the viceroys and subordinate officials, alarmed though they were over the decline of the Indian population made evident in every new count, to refuse more than token obedience to royal orders from Spain for lightening the burdens on the Indian population. Accordingly, such great royal projects of reform as the cédulas of November 24, 1601 and May 26, 1609 remained virtually dead letters.[109]

Meanwhile, the owners of enterprises denied labor under the repartimiento, plus some of those given repartimiento labor but dissatisfied with the instability and insufficiency of a labor force changing weekly, were turning to an entirely different means of securing workers. This was so-called free wage labor. Under this system the worker, ostensibly of his own volition, hired himself out to an employer for wages and could leave at any time. Actually, from the beginning, such labor seems to have been closely associated with debt bondage, the worker being bound to serve by advances of money, food, and clothing. Under Spanish law the worker could not leave his employer until he had worked out his debt within the limits that such advances were permissible.[110]

The discussion of this development in colonial labor systems presents some difficulties of terminology both in English and Spanish. The Spaniards designated free Indian laborers by a number of terms. *Naboria* (originally *naborí*), perhaps the earliest term, arose in the Caribbean islands at the beginning of the sixteenth century and was transplanted to New Spain. On the mainland it quickly became further Hispanized into *naborio*, and this by analogy with *labor* became *laborio* by the end of the seventeenth century. At the same time the term *peón*, which at the time of the Conquest meant a foot soldier in the Spanish army entitled to a lesser allotment of land (*peonía*), came to be applied to Indian wage workers during the course of the seventeenth century, and by the time of the Wars of Independence became the ordinary term used for a day laborer. During the nineteenth century peón came to mean a worker held by debt because of the almost universal use of the debt device to obtain and hold workmen; and with the adoption of the debt device to hold agricultural labor in our southern states after the Civil War, the word entered United States law to designate a worker held by debt, whence our legal terms peon and peonage. The term peón in post-sixteenth-century Mexican Spanish thus may mean indiscriminately both a free wage worker and a worker held by debt. In ordinary English the word peon also has both these Spanish uses. Only in United States law does it have a single explicit meaning. To avoid confusion, therefore, this study will use "naborio" for so-called free Indian wage laborers, and will make reference to the debt device clear by using the terms "debt peon" and "debt peonage."[111]

Free labor with its associated debt peonage must have developed in the Spanish colony in the first decades after the Conquest. By 1567 the use of debt to recruit and hold Indian labor was widespread enough to bring about a royal order to reform some of the more flagrant abuses of the method.[112] At the close of the sixteenth century a viceregal survey of mining showed the importance of naborios in that industry relative to both Negro slaves and repartimiento Indians. The mines of the Audiencia of Mexico and the Real de Zacatecas, which lay in the territory of the Audiencia of Guadalajara had the following labor force:

<pre>
            Negro slaves 1,022
            Naborios 4,606
            Repartimiento Indians 1,619
</pre>

Zacatecas received no Indians from repartimiento whatever.[113] It employed approximately 1,500 naborios.[114] These may be subtracted from the total for free Indian workmen to give the number in the Audiencia of Mexico alone. The mines in the southern audiencia thus employed 3,106 naborios as against 1,619 repartimiento Indians, a proportion of roughly two naborios to every repartimiento Indian. For the mines in the Audiencia of Guadalajara with fewer Indian towns to levy on, the proportion of wage laborers to repartimiento Indians must have been far larger. Even though figures are still lacking for agriculture, we may surmise that by the end of the sixteenth century the use of so-called free laborers was spreading rapidly in crop and stock raising although a large, perhaps the greater, proportion of workmen still was provided through operation of the repartimiento.[115] Almost certainly most of the naborios in both mining and agriculture were held by debt.

Debt peonage had substantial advantages for the Spanish employer. While avoiding the large investment needed for Negro slaves, it secured the stable supply of labor which the repartimiento with its weekly shift and shrinking yield could not provide. As compared to the 6.3 per cent or less of the annual time of the adult male Indian laborers, which the repartimiento could get from the Indian towns, debt peonage made available all or most of the time of the Indians secured as laborers. (The employer had to provide keep for his laborers under either system.)[116]

The development of debt peonage met only limited resistance from the royal government. The crown regarded free wage labor as the best possible system if the Indians could be brought to present themselves in sufficient numbers to meet the labor demand.[117] It was especially anxious to have a class of free laborers developed at the mines. Those tributaries who were willing to go to the mines as wage laborers were free in 1582 from all payment of tributes.[118] Nor did the crown object to a moderate use of debt in recruiting and holding Indian laborers. Its officials hunted down and returned fugitive debtors to their masters with no rebuke, overt or implied, from the viceregal administrators or the court in Madrid.[119] The crown's regulatory efforts derived from a policy of preventing contract labor based on debt from becoming another form of slavery or serfdom with the latter's implied reëstablishment of feudal privileges. Crown officials therefore attempted to fix three, then four, months' wages without continuing loans as the limit for advances in agriculture and eight months' wages as the limit for advances in mining. They also forbade employers to use coercive measures to get Indians to incur debt.[120] Their efforts aroused stubborn resistance among local employers, who were determined to acquire a fixed and stable labor supply, and who were able to persuade many of the local officials both Spanish and Indian to overlook infractions of the ordinances or even to assist them directly in securing workmen.

A number of the rules and arrangements adopted by the viceregal government actually aided materially in developing and extending debt peonage. A series of ordinances and decisions forbade the *sonsaque,* that is, the luring away of laborers by another employer.[121] These decisions carried the prohibition to the point of forbidding an employer-creditor who sold his property from taking his laborers with him. He must be reimbursed for the debts, but the laborers passed with the property to the new owner.[122] Despite the conventional fiction of free Indian labor, such rules obviously meant chaining the labor supply to the productive unit. The development of the new relationship was also furthered early in the seventeenth century by a new rule making the employer responsible for the payment to the crown of his workers' tribute.[123] The arrangement meant an annually recurring debt to the employer which had to be paid in labor. The royal treasury officials were interested only in assuring payment of revenue, but the rule assisted materially in breaking the ties of the Indian workers to their towns and aided the Spanish in binding them to their enterprises.

Debt peonage developed rapidly as an institution during the seventeenth century. Documents of the middle of the century already refer to naborios born on the estates where they worked, presumably the children of naborios. Later in the century, use of the term *terrazgueros* indicated the presence of laborers living on latifundia who were given use of some land as part payment for services. Both terms point to the existence of agricultural estates drawing their labor supply largely from Indians settled within their boundaries; it was these who passed with the estate to a new owner. By the end of the seventeenth century, owners of estates referred to such laborers and their families as *adscripticios;* that is, *adscripti ad glebam,* the late Roman and medieval term for serfs. Use of this term meant a claim rather than a legally established right, but the landholders with the connivance of local officials were in a good position to enforce their claim.[124]

The history of the repartimiento during the seventeenth century indicates that debt peonage had become the major source of labor. In 1632 the Marquis de Cerralvo, then viceroy, ordered the repartimiento abolished except to provide labor for the mines, which needed all the labor they could secure from whatever source.[125] His order also was not enforced for public works. Mining and public works were the exceptions which continued to draw labor by repartimiento almost to the end of the colonial period.[126] In agriculture, implementation of the order of 1632 was a fairly slow process taking place district by district as the local landholders and other employers felt secure in possession of a sufficient supply of labor.[127] By the end of the seventeenth century, use of the repartimiento continued in agriculture under the flimsy disguise of orders to persuade Indians from the Indian villages to accept paid employment, but it was resorted to only in peak seasons or in emergencies to supplement the labor force maintained on the estates.[128]

By the end of the seventeenth century, debt peonage also figured largely in the supply of labor for spinning and weaving establishments and the furnishing of labor in other skilled crafts. It probably developed in these as early as it appeared in mining and agriculture. The development of debt peonage also meant that employers possessed a device that could be used to bind mestizos and other groups which until then had been exempt from forced service. The demographic recovery of the end of the seventeenth century and the eighteenth century, as has already been pointed out, involved the growth of a large and increasing group of mestizos and mixed bloods, most of whom were not subject to tribute or compulsory service as were the Indians. As the group developed, the crown bureaucracy looked longingly upon them as an element which should justly be held to labor, particularly when labor was so short and the mixed bloods merely served to swell the new *lépero* class of outcasts, beggars, and starving dwellers in the slums and streets. But a large number of mixed bloods successfully evaded efforts of crown officials to turn them into worthy, law-abiding workmen. In addition, the population development of the middle colonial period also meant the emergence of an increasingly large group of poor Spanish (probably also mestizo but considered Spanish), many of whom were distinguished from the lépero class, I suspect, only by their pride. By the early decades of the eighteenth century, the debt device was gradually being extended to bind into service many of the mixed bloods who had hitherto evaded service, and even poor Spanish.[129] By this time, too, a reverse process was taking place through the amalgamation of part of the Indian nobility into the Spanish upper class. A number of Indians owned Spanish-style farms and spinning and weaving establishments operated with debt-held labor.[130]

Through debt peonage the upper stratum of the Mexican population thus largely solved the serious labor problem which began in 1576–1579. This solution was so advanced by the early eighteenth century that the British South Sea Company found New Spain a poor market for slaves introduced under the *Asiento* of 1715. In 1736 the manager of the Veracruz trading post reported to the London headquarters of the company:

With regard to the Negro trade of Vera Cruz tho' the prices there are the best..., yet no settlement the Company have made has had a smaller demand for slaves owing to the vast number of tributary Indians w'th which the Kingdom of New Spain abounds who perform all labour at easy rates. Since the first settlement of the factory in 1715 to the time of my leaving it the whole number Introduc'd amounted only to 2449 heads and none [of] the Provinces of Yucatan, Tabasco, Guatemala have been supplied by the Campechy Introductions. The demands at Vera Cruz are become less...[131]

By this time the cheapness of labor by debt peons largely confined the use of Negro slaves to domestic service, where their function was as much display of their master's wealth as performance of work.

Debt peonage did not emerge as the dominant form of labor relationship without a good deal of resistance. The limited efforts of the crown have already been mentioned. The encomendero class, which found its tributaries drifting away and its revenues correspondingly restricted, fought to keep laborers in the jurisdiction of its towns except for those encomenderos who were establishing their own estates and preferred to have their tributaries become debt peons. The most decided resistance came from the Indian towns. For them the drift to mines and agricultural estates meant a serious loss of people to help meet tribute and labor quotas. The outward movement of laborers and their families also meant a smaller group available to meet levies for the caciques, community treasuries, and the local religious cult. Although the Indian towns were able to secure rulings, especially in the sixteenth and first half of the seventeenth century, that town members accepting wage employment must return to take their turn in the repartimiento and must pay tributes through the town, they were unable to interfere materially with the extraction of laborers from their midst to form the new group of debt peons. Early in the seventeenth century, when the employers became responsible for collection of tributes, the Indian towns lost perhaps their major hold on their former members.[132]

The formation of the large debt peon group thus meant destruction of town or tribal control over a part of the Indian population. The laborers removed from the continuing centers of Indian culture were settled in centers of Spanish influence, where they would tend to adopt Spanish as their language, intermarry with other tribes or with mixed bloods, and become absorbed in the emerging hybrid Mexican culture. Debt peonage, ironically, helped to forge the Mexican nation.

One further comment remains to be made on debt peonage. Colonial labor relations were often attended by oppression, cruelty, and exploitation. However, debt peonage did not necessarily mean a downward step for the laborer. If he was bound to an employer, he was at least reserved for the service of that employer and protected to a considerable measure from the extortions to which he had been subject as a member of an Indian community. He was no longer required to assist in supporting the oppressive Indian nobility and the often elaborate and expensive community activities. If the local friars or secular priests were minded to make use of his services, they had to contend with the employer-creditor, who was not likely to permit inroads upon his labor supply. Furthermore, if only as a necessary worker, the debt peon probably got protection against exactions by itinerant Spaniards and local officials, who often added extra burdens to Indian life in the native towns. It is thus entirely conceivable that debt peonage meant an improvement in the life of many of the laborers. Such a view derives some support, although the evidence is scanty indeed, from the slow but accelerating upswing in population which began in the last decades of the seventeenth century. This upswing was due not only to a growing immunity to European epidemics, but also to an increase in the size of the natural family from the 3.2 of the middle sixteenth century to a figure near five by the end of the seventeenth century, and by the eighteenth century nearer to six. This increase presupposes such an improvement in living conditions, wretched though these continued to be, as to increase individual resistance and lower the ordinary infant and adult death rates. A further bit of evidence pointing to improvement in the status of the naborios is the fact that the Indian towns participated in this upswing later and at a slower rate than the mestizo element.

The measures adopted by the white population of New Spain to meet the shortage of labor and supplies thus involved sharp curtailment in the use of labor, the rapid development of large agricultural properties raising food for the cities, and the eventual adoption of debt peonage as the basic means of securing labor, supplemented to some extent by continuation of the earlier repartimiento. Until a great deal of further research is done on these points, any discussion of the effectiveness of these measures must be conjectural. The funneling of labor to more essential activities would certainly have helped substantially in any situation of severe shortage. The development of latifundia would have made much more efficient use of whatever Indian labor was available for food supply. Its effectiveness depended upon the extent to which first the repartimiento and later debt peonage could secure enough labor from the Indian population to man the latifundia as well as other Spanish enterprises. Probably even at the low point of the population, approximately 1,500,000 about 1650, there were enough Indians available to man all essential services and even to provide a considerable margin of labor if a fairly large proportion of the Indians' working time could have been secured for the white population. In agriculture and stock-raising, the Spanish cities, despite periods of stringency and even of near-famine, apparently did manage to feed themselves and to provide for a growing white population. Their most difficult period of shortage may have been the 1620's and 1630's when a prolonged series of bad crop years and the enormous labor demand of the Huehuetoca drainage canal complicated an already vexing problem.

For mining, comment on the success of the measures taken to solve the labor crisis is made far more difficult by the fact that by the 1580's the Mexican mines had run through the rich surface deposits and were processing less easily worked ore. They were faced not merely with the difficulty of securing labor, but also with the problem of obtaining mercury and other supplies and of draining their mines as the shafts reached the water line. The chief product, silver, brought a fixed return of approximately one peso an ounce at the same time that prices were rising for labor, food, fodder, and for most of the supplies the mines had to use. The prosperity or decline of the mines thus involved the operation of a complex series of cost and tax factors.[133] The scanty evidence available on mining output[134] provides our only clue to the extent of success in solving these problems. In general the period 1575–1600 showed a continuing expansion of output until a peak in the decade 1591–1600. From this high level output slowly declined until 1630. From 1631 to 1660, the decline was precipitous. At some time after 1660 mining output began to rise fairly rapidly, until by the early years of the 1690's it was approaching the yields of the 1580's. During the whole of the eighteenth century output increased fairly steadily and rapidly.[135] On the basis of output we may conjecture that the viceregal government was successful in providing labor and supplies at low enough prices for the mines during the 1580's and 1590's. Shortage of labor was probably a major factor in the decline following 1600, although difficulties in supplies of mercury and other items undoubtedly figured in it, as did the technological problem of drainage. Shortage of labor probably explains also the decision of the viceregal government to retain the repartimiento as a means of finding labor for the mines. The changes in labor systems therefore were less successful in meeting the needs of mining than in maintaining food production and other forms of economic activity.

CONCLUSION

The sharp and long-continued decrease of Mexico's Indians from the Conquest until the beginning of the eighteenth century must be accounted one of the most important factors in Mexican history. Had the aboriginal populations of central Mexico borne the impact of Conquest with little demographic loss, there would have been scant room for their conquerors except as administrators and receivers of tribute. Mexico today would be an Indian area from which, in the process of achieving independence from Spain, a white upper stratum holding itself apart, like the British in India, could easily have been expelled. In Haiti, expulsion and massacre at the time of the great slave uprisings disposed rather easily of a similar group of owners and administrators.

The hypothesis of a century-long depression developed in this paper can only be established by further research in Mexican economic and social history. If this hypothesis is sound, the precipitate and sustained decrease in the Indian hewers of wood and drawers of water after the demographic plateau of 1546–1576, the years when the white upper stratum became firmly established in the colony, confronted the new dominant group with one of the most severe and difficult problems of the colonial period. The problem was made more difficult by the fact that the Spanish actually increased steadily as the Indians diminished. The efforts of the Spanish to solve the problem, to continue to draw products and services in accustomed volume from the Indian understrata, speeded up and perhaps led directly to a radical reorganization of land holding and labor forms which greatly extended and strengthened the emerging hybrid Mexican culture. At the end of the seventeenth century, the distinctively Mexican economy was already organized on the basis of latifundia and debt peonage, the twin aspects of Mexican life which continued nearly to our day and which helped provoke the Revolution of 1910–1917.

NOTES

NOTES

[1] "Edelmetall-Produktion und Werthverhältniss zwischen Gold und Silber seit Entdeckung Amerikas bis zur Gegenwart," *Petermann's Mittheilungen*, XIII, No. 57 (Gotha, 1879), pp. 49–60.

[2] "Es ist ferner einleuchtend, dass die Berechnung der Edelmetall-Produktion als etwa das Fünffache der für Rechnung der Krone remittirten baaren Summen offenbar zu grosse Beträge herausstellen würde. Im Zeitraum von 1581 bis 1587 sind jährlich aus Mexiko nach Spanien für den Fiskus nahezu 932 000 Pesos geschickt, was als Quinto genommen, ohne Zuschlag für Defraudation, eine Produktion von 4 660 000 Pesos voraussetzen würde. Da nun ungefähr hundert Jahre später, wo die uns erhaltenen genauen Angaben über die gesammten Mexikanischen Ausmünzungen anfangen, die durchschnittliche jährliche Edelmetall-Produktion in Mexiko auf höchstens 4 600 000 Pesos zu schätzen ist, und da sämmtliche Berichte darin übereinstimmen, was auch an sich sehr wahrscheinlich ist, dass die Silber-Gewinnung in Mexiko im Verlaufe des siebenzehnten Jahrhunderts eine allmähliche Ausdehnung erfahren habe und also gegen Ende des sechzehnten Jahrhunderts wesentlich niedriger gewesen sein muss, so ist es klar, dass Mexiko 1571 bis 1580 und 1581 bis 1587 im Jährlichen Durchschnitte noch nicht einen gleich beträchtlichen Werthbetrag an Silber und Gold hat liefern können wie hundert Jahre später." *Ibid.*, pp. 52–53.

[3] "Beiträge zur Statistik der Edelmetalle," *Jahrbücher für Nationalökonomie und Statistik*, XXXIV (Jena, 1879), pp. 380–390.

[4] Mexico, Secretaría de la economía nacional, Dirección general de estadística, *Anuario estadístico de los Estados Unidos Mexicanos, 1942* (Mexico City, 1948), pp. 933– 937; Mexico, Secretaría de la economía nacional, Departamento de minas, *Anuario de estadística minera. Año de 1933* (Mexico City, 1938), pp. 24–25.

[5] Alfred Louis Kroeber, "Native American Population," *American Anthropologist*, XXXVI (1934), 1–25; Miguel Othón de Mendizábal, "La Demografía mexicana. Epoca colonial 1519–1810. Demografía colonial del siglo XVI, 1519–1599," *Obras completas* (6 vols. Mexico City, 1946–1947), III, 307–335; George Kubler, "Population Movements in Mexico," *The Hispanic American Historical Review*, XXII (1942), 606–643; Angel Rosenblat, *La Población indígena de América desde 1492 hasta la actualidad* (Buenos Aires, 1945); Gonzalo Aguirre Beltrán, *La Población negra de México, 1519–1810,* (Mexico City, 1946), esp. pp. 199–245; George Kubler, *Mexican Architecture of the Sixteenth Century* (2 vols., New Haven, Yale University Press, 1948), I, 23–53; Sherburne F. Cook and Lesley Byrd Simpson, *The Population of Central Mexico in the Sixteenth Century* (Univ. Calif. Ibero-Americana: 31, Berkeley, 1948). Aguirre Beltrán is concerned with the development of Negro elements and admixtures in the population after the Conquest. The other writers deal with aboriginal population. Mendizábal, Rosenblat, Kubler, and Cook and Simpson differ among themselves about numbers but not about the general trend. Kubler, who postulates a partial recovery among the Indians, involving a rising population for the thirty years between 1546 and 1576, agrees on the serious and continuing downward demographic movement after 1576.

[6] Mendizábal, *op. cit.*, pp. 332–333.

[7] Cook and Simpson, *op. cit.*, pp. 17–18. In this work the authors suggest that the birth rate actually fell: "A low family number implies not only a high death rate resulting from disease and poor living conditions, but also a relatively low birth rate." However, the work of Cook on Indian populations in the California missions indicates that under similar conditions of decline in an aboriginal population, the birth rate in terms of children per adult female remained relatively unchanged. The decline was brought about by a rise in the death rate of infants, children, and adults. Sherburne F. Cook, *Population Trends among the California Mission Indians* (Univ. Calif. Ibero-Americana: 17, Berkeley, 1940), *passim*, esp. p. 48.

[8] Cook and Simpson, *op. cit.*, pp. 16, 18–48. The continuing decline in Indian numbers during the early decades of the seventeenth century is further clearly brought out in the careful discussion for New Galicia by François Chevalier in his introduction to Domingo Lázaro de Arregui, *Descripción de la Nueva Galicia* (Seville, 1946), pp. xlix–l, and in a report of the

Marqués de Cerralvo to the king on his administration as viceroy, Mexico City, March 17, 1636, in Fray Antonio Vázquez de Espinosa, *Descripción de la Nueva España en el siglo XVII ... y otros documentos del siglo XVII ...* , ed. by Mariano Cuevas (Mexico City, 1944), p. 227.

[9] See Sherburne F. Cook, "The Population of Mexico in 1793," *Human Biology*, XIV (December, 1942), 499–515, for an analysis of the development of mixed-blood elements in the population of New Spain. Also see below. Increase among non-Indians and mixed-bloods was probably due to the two factors of lower death rate and recruiting from the Indian mass rather than to any substantial difference in the birth rate.

[10] The efforts on the part of the viceregal administrations to bring together scattered Indian hamlets into compact towns, the so-called policy of *congregación,* meant *inter alia* an attempt to reduce the burden of religious cult and village governments. For a study of the operation of this policy in the late sixteenth and early seventeenth century, see Lesley Byrd Simpson, *Studies in the Administration of the Indians in New Spain. Part Two: The Civil Congregation* (Univ. Calif. Ibero-Americana: 7, Berkeley, 1934).

[11] The presence of non-Spanish Europeans is clearly evident in grants and other documents in Archivo General de la Nación, Mexico, Mercedes, I–X, *passim* (this archive is cited hereafter as AGN), and in the records of prosecutions for heresy by the Inquisition. José Toribio Medina, *Historia del tribunal del santo oficio de la Inquisición en México* (Santiago, Chile, 1905), *passim.*

[12] See, for example, the description of Acuitlapan in *Descripción del arzobispado de México hecha en 1570 y otros documentos,* ed. by Luis García Pimentel (Mexico City, 1897), pp. 131–132. The corresponding description of the town of Antequera (now Oaxaca City) states that one-third of the *vecinos* were married to mestizo or mulatto women. *Relación de los obispados de Tlaxcala, Michoacán, Oaxaca y otros lugares en el siglo XVI, manuscrito de la colección del Señor Don Joaquín García Icazbalceta ...* (Mexico City, 1904), p. 69. There was thus some admixture of Negro blood as well although in far smaller proportion.

[13] Cook, "The Population of Mexico in 1793," *Human Biology*, XIV (December, 1942), 500–504.

[14] This use of the term vecinos is clearly evident in the accounts in the *Descripción del arzobispado de México* and the *Relación de los obispados de Tlaxcala, Michoacán, Oaxaca y otros lugares.* In addition, see the accounts cited below. Vecino was also applied to Indian heads of households in describing or counting the aboriginal population.

[15] See Pedro Alonso O'Crouley (1774), "Ydea compendiosa del Reyno de Nueva España en que se comprehenden las Ciudades y Puertos principales, Cabezeras de Jurisdiccion, su Latitud, Rumbo, y distancia a la Capital, Mexico. señalanse los principales Presidios y Guarniciones: con circunstanciada Descripcion de las partes mas remotas y menos conocidas; . . ." (Madrid, Biblioteca Nacional, MS 4532). Kubler, *Mexican Architecture of the Sixteenth Century,* I, 71, uses this factor of five.

[16] See the discussion on the size of the Indian family in Cook and Simpson, *op. cit.,* pp. 17–18.

[17] *Descripción del arzobispado de México* and *Relación de los obispados de Tlaxcala, Michoacán, Oaxaca y otros lugares, passim.*

[18] *Geografía y descripción universal de las Indias, recopilada por el cosmógrafo-cronista ... desde el año de 1571 al de 1574,* ed. by Justo Zaragoza (Madrid, 1894).

[19] *Ibid.,* p. 187.

[20] *Ibid.,* p. 189.

[21] *Ibid.,* p. 209.

[22] "Descripción del obispado de Antequera, de la Nueva España, hecha por el obispo del dicho obispado, por mandado de S. M.," *ca.* 1570, in *Relación de los obispados de Tlaxcala, Michoacán, Oaxaca y otros lugares,* p. 61.

[23] AGN, Archivo del Hospital de Jesús, *passim.*

[24] López de Velasco, *op. cit.,* p. 187.

[25] Juan Díez de la Calle, *Memorial y noticias sacras y reales del imperio de las Indias Occidentales ...* ([Madrid], 1646).

[26] *Ibid.,* fol. 45ʳ–45ᵛ.

[27] O'Crouley, *op. cit.,* fols. 36–38.

[28] *Theatro americano, descripción general de los reynos, y Provincias de la Nueva-España, y sus jurisdicciones* ... (2 vols. Mexico City, 1746–1748). Alexander von Humboldt, writing at a more advanced stage in the development of statistics, rather unkindly characterized the excerpts in Villaseñor as being "as incomplete as inexact." *Essai politique sur le royaume de la Nouvelle-Espagne* ... (5 vols. Paris, 1811), I, 323 (Bk. II, chap. iv). He apparently based his comment upon the fact that the 1742 count used the older method of estimating families rather than individuals and upon the failure of Villaseñor to reproduce all of the information. This failure may have been intentional.

[29] AGN, Reales cédulas, LXXXV, fol. 142, cited in Aguirre Beltrán, *op. cit.*, p. 224.

[30] This value is based upon an estimate of 10,000–12,000 for all clergy, white and of other races.

[31] Compare the totals for the bishoprics of Michoacán and Nueva Galicia in tables 7 and 8.

[32] O'Crouley, *op. cit.*

[33] This would imply a total for clergy of all categories of perhaps 10,000. Humboldt, *op. cit.*, II, 31–32 (Bk. II, chap. vii) suggests 13,000–14,000 as the number of clergy in New Spain in 1793.

[34] *Ibid.*, I, 325 (Bk. II, chap. iv).

[35] *Ibid.*, I, 326–327 (Bk. II, chap. iv).

[36] Cook and Simpson, *op. cit.*, p. 48.

[37] Cook, "The Population of Mexico in 1793," *Human Biology*, XIV (December, 1942), 503.

[38] "Memoria sobre la población del reino de Nueva-España ... ," Sociedad mexicana de geografía y estadística, *Boletín*, 2ª ep., I (1869), 281–291, esp. 288.

[39] Humboldt, *op. cit.*, II, 459 (Bk. III, chap. viii).

[40] That is 112,926 plus one-sixth. Humboldt, *op. cit.*, I, 325 (Bk. II, chap. vii). The markedly larger figures in earlier estimates for the white population of the capital are explained by the fact that the earlier counts included the people in the administrative district directly associated with the capital and vecinos admitted to local citizenship although residing elsewhere. The census of 1790–1793 defined Mexico City as being only the urban center.

[41] Humboldt, *op. cit.*, II, 60 (Bk. II, chap. vii).

[42] *Ibid.*, II, 8 (Bk. II, chap. vii).

[43] *Ibid.*, II, 459 (Bk .III, chap. viii). The break-down for all elements is as follows:

Indians	2,500,000
Whites	1,095,000
Negroes	6,100
Mixed Bloods	1,231,000
	4,832,100

Humboldt elsewhere (II, 8, Bk. II, chap. vii) gives 1,200,000 as the number of white persons. This may be a calculation of the number in 1803.

[44] *Ibid.*, I, 325–340 (Bk. II, chap. iv) and II, 111–459 (Bk. III, chap. viii).

[45] *Ibid.*, I, 344–345 (Bk. II, chap. v) and II, 304 (Bk. III, chap. viii); Cook, "The Population of Mexico in 1793," *Human Biology*, XIV (December, 1942), 513–515.

[46] Copia de los advertimientos que el virrey don Luis de Velasco dexó al Conde de monteRey para el gouierno de la nueua España, *ca.* November, 1595, MS in Archivo General de Indias, Seville, 58–3–13, Bancroft Library Transcript (this archive is cited hereafter as AGI and Bancroft Library Transcripts cited as BLT); Royal cédula to the Marqués de Guadalcázar, Madrid, December 12, 1669, MS in AGN, Reales cédulas, duplicados, VI, fols. 2ᵛ–5ʳ (BLT). Alonso de la Mota y Escobar has a striking phrase: "los yndios cuyo sudor haze ricos a los españoles ..." *Descripción geográfica de los reynos de Galicia, Vizcaya y León* ... (Mexico City, 1930), p. 100.

[47] Alonso de Zorita, *Historia de la Nueva España ... tomo primero* ... , (Madrid, 1909), pp. 193–194; order of the Conde de Monterrey to the juez repartidor of the city of Valladolid, Mexico, December 11, 1599, in Silvio A. Zavala and María Castelo, comps., *Fuentes para la historia del trabajo en Nueva España* ... (8 vols., Mexico City, 1939–[1946]), IV, 380–381.

[48] *Memoriales ... , manuscrito de la colección del Señor Don Joaquín García Icazbalceta ...* ed. by Luis García Pimentel (Mexico City, 1903), pp. 24–25.

[49] Resumen de los autos del pleito seguido por los indios de Coyoacán, en contra de Don Martín Cortés y de su padre Don Hernando, sobre casas, huerta, tierras y servicios personales en los villas de Coyoacán, Tacubaya, y en la ciudad de México, [1561 ?], *Documentos inéditos relativos a Hernan Cortes y su familia* (AGN, *Publicaciones*, XXVII (1935), pp. 351–352.

[50] Alonso de Zorita, *Breve y sumaria relación de los señores de la Nueva España ...* (Mexico City, 1942), pp. 138–149; Kubler, *Mexican Architecture of the Sixteenth Century*, I and II, *passim*, but esp. I, 148–151, II, 535. For a description of the church and convent of Yanhuitlán, see Manuel Toussaint, *Paseos coloniales* (Mexico City, 1939), pp. 63–78.

[51] Aguirre Beltrán, *op. cit.*, pp. 4–7, 11–12, 15, *et passim*. Enríquez to the king, Mexico City, March 20, 1580, MS in AGI, 58–3–9 (BLT).

[52] MS in AGI, 58–3–9 (BLT).

[53] Order of the Marqués de Villamanrrique assigning Jerónimo López fifteen Indians from the town of Axacuba, Mexico City, July 3, 1587, in Zavala and Costelo, *op. cit.*, III, 43–44.

[54] AGN, General de Parte, I–III, *passim*. Other examples of such orders extracted by Zavala and Castelo from AGN are: order issued by the Conde de Coruña that Melchior López Castellanos, miner of Pachuca, be allotted Indians from the repartimiento of Cempoala, Mexico City, December 2, 1580; and orders of the Conde de Coruña that Pedro de Quero, silversmith preparing lead for ships on the Pacific coast be allotted services of two Indians, Mexico City, December 14, 1580 and January 12, 1581. *Op. cit.*, II, 376–377, 383–384, and 392.

[55] Zorita, *Historia*, pp. 193–194; Zorita, *Breve y sumaria relación*, pp. 177–209; Velasco II to the king, Mexico City, April 6, 1595, MS in AGI, 58–3–12 (BLT); Ordinances against regrating in maize and wheat, Mexico City, October 15, November 10, and November 17, 1579 and January 11, 1583, MSS in AGN, Reales cédulas, duplicados, XIV, fols. 129–136 (BLT).

[56] MS in AGN, 58–3–12 (BLT). Velasco II urged as one means of handling this situation that white immigration to New Spain be sharply curtailed: "Asi mismo he significado a Vuestra Magestad en carta de 25 de junio de 92 años los muchos y notables daños e ynconuinientes que se siguen de dexar passar a estas partes tanta gente como passa por que no uiene flota que no dexe aca sobre 800 personas hombres y mugeres unos que traen licencias y otros sin ellas y como hallan la comida facilmente que ya no ay otra riqueza en la nueua españa aunque tampoco es como solia ninguna se aplica a servir ni trauajar ni quieren y andan las plaças y calles llenas de mugeres baldias y hombres bagabundos perdidos y perdidas que no se ocupan sino en comer y jugar y en otros peores vicios con que ynficionan la tierra y la traen ynquieta ..." Letter to the king, Mexico City, April 6, 1594, MS in AGI, 58–3–12 (BLT).

[57] Copia de los advertimientos que el Virrey don Luis de Velasco dexó al Conde de monteRey para el gouierno de la nueua España, *ca.* November, 1595, MS in AGI, 58–3–13 (BLT). Other descriptions, reports, and comments either on the food situation in general or on difficulties in supply at one time are: Instrucción y advertimientos quel virey D. Martín Enríquez dejó al Conde de Coruña, September 25, 1580, in *Instrucciones que los vireyes de Nueva España dejaron a sus sucesores. Añadense algunos que los mismos trajeron de la corte y otros documentos semejantes a las instrucciones* (2 vols., Mexico City, 1873), I, 247; memorial of Villamanrrique to the king, n.d., MS in AGI, 58–3–11 (BLT); Velasco II to the king, Mexico City, October 5, 1593, MS in AGI, 58–3–11 (BLT); summary of a letter from Velasco II to the king, Mexico City, January 14, 1594, MS in AGI, 58–3–11 (BLT); Velasco II to the king, Mexico City, October 25, 1594, MS in AGI, 58–3–11 (BLT); Conde de Monterrey to the king, Mexico City, May 20, 1601, MS in AGI, 58–3–13 (BLT); Velasco II to the king, Mexico City, February 13, 1609, MS in AGI, 58–3–16 (BLT); Conde de Priego to the king, Mexico City, February 26, 1622, in Vazquez de Espinosa, *op. cit.*, p. 216. See also the order of the Marqués de Villamanrrique that Indians assigned to work on the cathedral church of Puebla de Los Angeles be paid one real for food above ordinary wages because of the poor corn harvest, Mexico City, June 20, 1587; order of Velasco the Younger to the juez repartidor of Tacubaya for an emergency allotment of labor to save the wheat crop, Mexico City, October 26, 1590; order of Velasco II to the juez repartidor of the valley of Atlixco for the concentration of all labor available on the wheat

harvest, Mexico City, March 11, 1591; order of the Conde de Montesclaros providing extra labor for the wheat farms in the valley of Atlixco, Mexico City, December 30, 1603, all of these in Zavala and Castelo, *op. cit.*, III, 39, 96, 148; and V, 193–194 respectively. See also the ordinance of the Marqués de Cerralvo commuting tributes of Indian towns held by the crown to cash payments as a means of preventing hoarding of foodstuffs, Mexico City, September 28, 1627, MS in AGN, Reales cédulas, duplicados, IX, fols. 75ʳ–76ʳ (BLT). Raymond L. Lee, "Grain Legislation in Colonial Mexico 1575–1585," *The Hispanic American Historical Review*, XXVII (November, 1947), 647–660, is an excellent account of the emergency measures resulting from the great plague of the 1570's.

[58] The foundation of the *alhondiga* of Mexico City, the first in New Spain, is an interesting story in itself. Enríquez lent 8,000 ducats from his own pocket for the first purchases of wheat. Early in 1579 a similar granary called *pósito* was begun for maize. The two granaries were soon merged under a single administration, a simple measure since they were housed in nearby rooms in the city buildings. In January–February, 1581 the cabildo adopted ordinances to regulate the administration of the alhóndiga which were confirmed on March 31, 1583 by Philip II and incorporated in the *Recopilación de las Indias*. The Mexico City alhóndiga became, in effect, the model and prototype for similar granaries not only in New Spain but throughout the Spanish possessions in America. Notes of sessions of the Mexico City cabildo of November 24 and 28, December 5, 1578, January 9, 1579, April 18 and 26, July 18, October 14, and November 11, 1580, January 9, February 23, April 28, May 22, and June 12, 1581, in *Actas de cabildo del ayuntamiento de México* (77 vols., Mexico City, 1884–1905), VIII, 361–362, 364, 374, 430, 431, 443, 461, 463, 479, 481, 491, 496, 500; *Recopilación de leyes de los reynos de las Indias* (2d ed., 4 vols., Madrid, 1756), II, fols. 107ʳ–110ᵛ (Lib. IV, tít. XIV, leyes i–xix); Lee, *op. cit.*, pp. 654–659.

[59] Ordinance issued by the Audiencia of Mexico, February 7, 1579, and implementing measures, MSS in AGN, Reales cédulas, duplicados, XLVI, fols. 121–128 (BLT); Lee, *op. cit.*, pp. 652–654.

[60] June 3, 1578. On June 12, 1578 a similar ordinance was applied to the mining regions of Zacualpan, Temascaltepec, Sultepec, and Pachuca. MSS in AGN, Reales cédulas, duplicados, XLVI, fols. 110–114 (BLT); Lee, *op. cit.*, p. 652.

[61] October 29, 1578, MS in AGN, Reales cédulas duplicados, XLVI, fols. 110–114 (BLT).

[62] November 21, 1578, MS in AGN, Reales cédulas, duplicados, XLVI, fols. 115–120 (BLT); Lee, *op. cit.*, pp. 652–653.

[63] Ordinances of October 15, 1579, November 10, 1579, November 17, 1579, and January 11, 1583, MSS in AGN, Reales cédulas, duplicados, XLVI, fols. 129–136 (BLT); ordinances of July 31, 1583, January 22, 1594, January 29, 1598, December 11, 1604, March 16, 1612, November 18, 1615, November 28, 1615, August 19, 1617, August 17, 1619, October 24, 1623, March 20, 1666, MSS in AGN, Ordenanzas, I, fols. 80ᵛ–81ʳ, 143ʳ–143ᵛ; II, fols. 69ᵛ–70ʳ, 161ᵛ–162ʳ; III, 2ᵛ–5ʳ, 17ᵛ–24ᵛ, 52ᵛ–53ʳ (BLT). Parts of some of these ordinances and sections of others are compiled in Juan Francisco de Montemayor y Córdova de Cuenca, *Svmarios de las cedvlas, ordenes y provisiones reales, que se han despachado por Su Magestad, para la Nueva-España, y otras partes; especialmente desde el año de mil seiscientos y veinte y ocho ... Con algvnos titvlos de las materias, qve nuevamente se añaden: y de los autos acordados de su Real audiencia ...* (Mexico City, 1678), Pt. III, ordinances 11, 12, 13, 14, 15, 51, 94, 96, 97, 98, 130.

[64] Order of the Marqués de Cerralvo for information on the complaint of the farmers of Tacuba, Tacubaya, February 11, 1632, in Zavala and Castelo, *op. cit.*, VI, 562–563.

[65] Order of the Marqués de Cerralvo that additional laborers be provided the farmers of the valley of Atlixco, Mexico City, April 5, 1632, in Zavala and Castelo, *op. cit.*, VI, 568–569.

[66] See discussion by François Chevalier in Arregui, *op. cit.*, pp. lxviii–lxix.

[67] Woodrow Borah, "Tithe Collection in the Bishopric of Oaxaca, 1601–1867," *The Hispanic American Historical Review*, XXIX (November, 1949), 502–503.

[68] Arregui, *op. cit.*, pp. lxviii–lxix, 120; Mota y Escobar, *op. cit.*, pp. 54–55. See also the comments of Velasco II quoted above.

[69] Miguel Othón de Mendizábal, "La minería y la metalurgía mexicanas (1520–1943)," *Obras completas,* V, 34–36; order for a reduced allotment of Indians for the mines of Pachuca, Mexico City, in Zavala and Castelo, *op. cit.,* II, 347–349. There is a discrepancy of 20 between the village quotas, which add to 691, and the total of 711 in the order.

[70] Order of Viceroy Montesclaros for a revised allotment of Indian laborers for the mines of Pachuca, Mexico City, January 23, 1607, in Zavala and Castelo, *op. cit.,* VI, 117–120.

[71] Order of the Marqués de Leyva, Mexico City, July 1, 1661, in Zavala and Castelo, *op. cit.,* VIII, 17–22.

[72] Instrucción y advertimientos cuel virey D. Martín Enríquez dejó al Conde de Coruña, September 25, 1580, *Instrucciones que los vireyes de Nueva España* ... I, 245; Villamanrrique to the king, Mexico City, May 10, 1586, MS in AGI, 58–3–9 (BLT); Velasco II to the king, Mexico City, October 30, 1591, MS in AGI, 58–3–11 (BLT); Velasco II to the king, Mexico City, February 25, 1593, MS in AGI, 58–3–11 (BLT); Velaso II to the king, Mexico City, October 5, 1593, MS in AGI, 58–3–11 (BLT); summary of a letter of Velasco II to the king, Mexico City, January 14, 1594, MS in AGI, 58–2–11 (BLT); Velasco II to the king, Mexico City, April 6, 1594, MS in AGI, 58–3–12 (BLT); Relación del estado que tienen las haziendas de minas de la nueua hespaña y de lo que a su magestad deuen ... , n.d. but early 1598, MS in AGI, 58–3–13 (BLT); [Conde de Monterrey] Advertimientos que ha parescido embiar a Vuestra Magestad Sobre el estado pressente de la real hazienda desta nueua hespaña ... , Mexico City, April 1, 1598, MS in AGI, 58–3–13 (BLT); Anonymous. Apuntamiento de las Vtilidades que parece se seguirán de que los yndios del Repartimiento de las minas Vayan a seruir a ellas por vn año y los ynconuinientes que en ello se an representado, n.d., MS in AGI, 58–3–13 (BLT); general orders of the Marqués de Cerralvo requiring enforcement of levies of Indian labor for the mines, Mexico City, December 30, 1625 and September 2, 1632, in Zavala and Castelo, *op. cit.,* VI, 608–609; order of the Marqués de Villena on provision of laborers for repairs, etc., to the mines of San Luis Potosí, Mexico City, January 31, 1642, in Zavala and Castelo, *op. cit.,* VII, 446–448; royal cédula to the Marqués de Guadalcázar, Madrid, December 12, 1669, MS in AGN, Reales cédulas, duplicados, VI, fols. 2ᵛ–5ʳ (BLT).

[73] Many of the complaints cited above make it clear that the shortage of labor was acute in all fields.

[74] Kubler, *Mexican Architecture of the Sixteenth Century,* I, 167–168, gives a striking instance of the rise of wages. In 1531 a *tapia* of rubble wall cost one peso for stone and labor together. At Izhuatepec in 1598 masons who built a similar extent of wall were paid fifteen pesos for labor alone. Most of the complaints of shortages listed above complain also of high prices.

[75] See pp. 43–44.

[76] Mexico City, December 22, 1590, MS in AGI, 58–3–11 (BLT). The effect of rising prices is discussed at some length by Zorita, *Breve y sumaria relación,* pp. 177–197. The encomenderos had some advantage in that part of their tributes were paid in maize.

[77] Unfortunately we still lack demographic studies based on tribute and parish counts for most of the Spanish colonies. George Kubler and John H. Rowe have contributed valuable studies for the area of the Incan Empire in the *Handbook of South American Indians,* II, 184–185 and 334–340 (Smithsonian Institution, Bureau of American Ethnology, Bulletin 143, Washington, 1946).

[78] Earl J. Hamilton, "The Decline of Spain," *Economic History Review,* VIII (May, 1938), 168–179, and Fernand Braudel, *La Méditerranée et le monde méditerranéen à l'époque de Philippe II* (Paris, 1949), pp. 354–358, on the basis of studies of urban population, place the beginning of the Spanish decline in the seventeenth century. Carmelo Viñas y Mey, *El problema de la tierra en la España de los siglos XVI–XVII* (Consejo superior de investigaciones ciéntificas, Instituto Jéronimo Zurita, Madrid, 1941), *passim,* shows that rural depopulation was well under way by the 1590's.

The nature of Spain's economic and demographic decline and the reasons for it have been discussed at some length by writers, but no attempt at explanation thus far is fully satisfactory. In addition to authors cited above, see the following works which are among the lengthier and more careful treatments: Maurice Ansiaux, "Histoire économique de la prosperité et de la décadence de l'Espagne au XVIe et au XVIIe siècles," *Revue d'économie politique,* VII (1893), 509–566, 1025–1059; Konrad Häbler, *Die wirtschaftliche Blüte Spaniens im 16. Jahrhundert und ihr Verfall* (Berlin, 1888); Julius Klein, *The Mesta. A Study in Spanish Economic History 1273–1836* (Harvard Economic Series, XXXI, Cambridge, Mass., 1920). Braudel, who re-examined the problem in a Mediterranean context (*op. cit., passim*) points out that Spain's decline was paralleled by economic difficulties and population loss in Italy and much of the Mediterranean basin as well as in some parts of northern Europe. His treatment raises questions which have not been adequately investigated, let alone answered.

[79] See Velasco II to the king, Mexico City, February 25, 1593, MS in AGI, 58–3–11 (BLT).

[80] See pp. 22–23.

[81] The last quarter of the sixteenth century and the early seventeenth century are the period of introduction into the colony of the *alcabala, bulas de la cruzada, composiciones de tierras,* sale of offices, general and forced loans, *medias anatas, mesadas,* stamped paper, extensions and increases in older levies such as tributes and the *almojarifazgo* and the establishment of state monopolies of salt, gunpowder, and mercury for mining, etc. See Fabián de Fonseca and Carlos de Urrutia, *Historia general de real hacienda ... escrita por orden del virrey, conde de Revillagigedo ...* (6 vols., Mexico City, 1845–1853), *passim.*

[82] Kubler, *Mexican Architecture of the Sixteenth Century,* I, 53–66.

[83] Such a conscious choice appears, for instance, in Villamanrrique to the king, Mexico City, February 23, 1583, MS in AGI, 58–3–9 (BLT). The choice lay between a sumptuous church in Coyoacán and a supply of artisans and laborers for the capital. The viceroy decided that the capital could not be deprived of its labor force.

[84] From 1573 to 1667 to be exact. Manuel Toussaint, "La catedral de México," in Gerardo Murillo, ed., *Iglesias de México* (6 vols., Mexico City, 1924–1927), II, 15–30. The preparation of the foundations in the marshy subsoil of Mexico City took from *ca.* 1558 to 1573.

[85] The requirement that each Indian tributary raise annually 12 hens, 1 rooster, and 6 turkeys was first issued by Enríquez. In 1617 it was reënacted by the Marqués de Guadalcázar. Ordinance of April 26, 1617, MS in AGN, Ordenanzas, III, fols. 39ᵛ–40ᵛ (BLT). See also Velasco II to the Council of the Indies, n.d., MS in AGI, 58–3–11 (BLT); Copia de los advertimientos que el Virrey don Luis de Velasco dexó al conde de monteRey para el gouierno de la nueua España, *ca.* November, 1595, MS in AGI, 58–3–13 (BLT); Conde de Monterrey to the king, Mexico City, May 26, 1601, MS in AGI, 58–3–13 (BLT); royal cédula to the Conde de Monterrey, Valladolid, November 24, 1601, MS in AGN, Reales cédulas, duplicados, LXIX, fol. 242ᵛ (BLT).

[86] Copia de los advertimientos que el Virrey don Luis de Velasco dexó al conde de monteRey para el gouierno de la nueua España, *ca.* November, 1595, MS in AGI, 58–3–13 (BLT).

[87] There was a considerable development of Spanish agriculture, especially in European crops like wheat, fruits, and livestock before 1576–1579 as is clearly evident from the grants in AGN, Mercedes, I–VIII, *passim,* but the major development would seem to have begun after the great epidemic of 1576–1579. Zorita, *Breve y sumaria relación,* pp. 148–149, mentioned the rapid increase in Spanish farms. Since he coupled this phenomenon with the decrease in Indians, presumably it took place concurrently with the decrease; that is, after Zorita's retirement to Spain. Even in retirement, Zorita apparently kept in touch wih developments in the colony.

Knowledge of the formation of large landed estates by the Spanish has been greatly extended through the remarkable study by François Chevalier, "La Naissance des grands domaines au Mexique xvie–xviiie siècles," MS, to be published by the University of Paris. (M. Chevalier very kindly permitted me to consult his only copy of the work.) He particularly stresses the role of tierras baldías in the formation of latifundia. The additional factors of market and the driving need of the cities are my own suggestion. For a fine study of a typical development of Spanish farms to feed a northern mining area, see Robert C. West, *The Mining Community in Northern New Spain: the Parral Mining District* (Univ. Calif. Ibero-Americana: 30, Berkeley, 1949), pp. 5–14, 57–76. Mota y Escobar, writing in 1603, clearly indicated the development of Spanish farms near the northern mines by that date (*op. cit., passim*).

[88] AGN, Mercedes, I–XII, *passim.*

[89] According to preliminary data from a study of land grants in central Mexico by Lesley Byrd Simpson, who very kindly made his tentative findings available for this paper.

[90] *Composición* meant both a settlement to clear title to land already held by the private party and payment for a grant of land. It is more usually used by historians in the first meaning. Chevalier, *op. cit.;* Velasco II to the Council of the Indies on proposals of the Junta de la Contaduría, n.d. but 1591–1593, MS in AGI, 58–3–11 (BLT); Relacion del estado que tenían Los atrassados de las Rentas Su Magestad tiene en estos Reynos de Nueua Spaña que se cobran en las Caxas de México, Çacatecas, Guadalaxara, y nueua Vizcaya fecho a 27 de Otubre de 1603 que empeco a Gouernar el Marqués de Montesclaros, MS in AGI, 58–3–15 (BLT); Gonzalo Aguirre Beltrán, *El Señorío de Cuauhtochco. Luchas agrarias en México durante el virreinato* (Mexico City, 1940), pp. 84–97; *Recopilación de leyes ... de Indias,* Lib. IV, tít. xii, leyes xiv, xv. Arregui, *op. cit.,* pp. 26–28, mentions that the Indians of Nueva Galicia tried to keep their lands by sending inhabitants from neighboring towns if necessary so that each town could claim occupancy of all lands it had held previously.

[91] Chevalier, *op. cit.;* Aguirre Beltrán, *El señorío de Cuahtochco* is a remarkable case history of the formation of Spanish latifundia in the canton of Huatusco (Huatusco being a corruption of Cuauhtochco, the aboriginal name for the area). The crown attempted to set some safeguards for the Indians in sales of property to Spanish. Royal cédula, Madrid, June 23, 1571, and royal cédula to the Audiencia of Mexico, Madrid, May 18, 1572, waiving application of the first cédula to sales of the value of 30 pesos or under because of the expense. (MSS in AGN, Reales cédulas, duplicados, XLVII, fol. 561^r–561^v [BLT].) On December 17, 1603 a new ordinance attempted to reintroduce safeguards for sales of lands by Indians even if the value of the property was no more than 30 pesos. Montemayor y Córdova de Cuenca, *op. cit.,* Pt. III, ordinance 134.

[92] Velasco II to the Council of the Indies on proposals of the Junta de la Contaduría, n.d. but 1591–1593, MS in AGI, 58–3–11 (BLT).

[93] Mota y Escobar, *op. cit.,* pp. 62–71.

[94] I am indebted to Professor Carl O. Sauer for this information.

[95] Lesley Byrd Simpson, *The Encomienda in New Spain. The Beginning of Spanish Mexico* (Berkeley and Los Angeles, University of California Press, 1950), pp. 167–169.

[96] Order of the Conde de Montesclaros providing extra labor for the valley of Atlixco, Mexico City, December 30, 1603, in Zavala and Castelo, *op. cit.,* V, 193–194.

[97] That is, in part, when the heavy labor demand for the Huehuetoca drainage canal fell off. Information on food production and supply is so scanty for most of the seventeenth century that any statement is little short of guessing. There was a long period of famine and near famine in the 1690's. See citations in note 98.

[98] Mendizébal, "La Demografía mexicana," in *Obras completas,* III, 326–329. Duque de Alburquerque to the king, Mexico City, March 31, 1703, MS in AGI, 61–1–23 (BLT).

[99] Instrucción y advertimientos quel virey D. Martín Enríquez dejó al Conde de Coruña ... , September 25, 1580, in *Instrucciones que los vireyes de Nueva España ... ,* I, 245; Villamanrrique to the king, Mexico City, May 10, 1586, MS in AGI, 58–3–9 (BLT); Velasco II to the king, Mexico City, October 5, 1593, MS in AGI, 58–3–11 (BLT); summary of a letter of Velasco II to the king, Mexico City, January 14, 1594, MS in AGI, 58–3–11 (BLT).

[100] Monterrey to the king, Mexico City, October 4, 1597, MS in AGI, 58–3–13 (BLT); Zavala and Castelo, *op. cit.,* IV, xvi–xxiv.

[101] Aguirre Beltrán, *La Población negra de México 1519–1810 ... ,* pp. 219–220 *et passim;* royal cédula to the Marqués de Guadalcázar, Madrid, December 12, 1669, MS in AGN, Reales cédulas, duplicados, VI, fols. 2^v–5^r (BLT).

[102] Zavala and Castelo, *op. cit.,* IV, xiv–xxiii, and introductions to Vols. V–VIII. Humboldt at the beginning of the nineteenth century remarked upon the general use of Indians in the sugar and cloth industries. The use of Indians for sugar production rather than Negroes as was customary in the Caribbean islands especially caught his attention (*op. cit.,* III, 176–177 [Bk. IV, chap. x] and IV, 290–296 [Bk. V, chap. xii]).

[103] Also called the *mita* in Peru, where the same system was adopted. Zavala and Castelo, *op. cit.*, introductions to Vols. I–IV, suggest *cuatequil* as a further term. This may, however, have referred only to the labor allocated to public works rather than to the system of levy. See Rémi Simeon, *Dictionnaire de la langue nahuatl ou mexicaine* (Paris, 1875) p. 101, and MSS in AGN, General de parte, I, *passim*. For descriptions of the repartimiento system of labor in detail, see Lesley Byrd Simpson, *Studies in the Administration of the Indians in New Spain. III: The Repartimiento System of Native Labor in New Spain and Guatemala,* (Univ. Calif. Ibero-Americana: 13, Berkeley, 1938); Zavala and Castelo, *op. cit.*, introductions to Vols. I–VIII, which contain a discussion of the development and history of the repartimiento in the form of a running commentary on the documents published in each volume; and Silvio A. Zavala, "Orígenes coloniales del peonaje en México," *Estudios indianos* (Mexico City, 1948), pp. 309–353, a reprint of an article first published in *El trimestre económico*, X (1944), 711–748.

My brief sketch of the repartimiento system differs on some points with the interpretation of Zavala and Castelo, especially the belief of these authors in the effectiveness of royal legislation, their stress on the value of the repartimiento relative to other systems in providing labor by the end of the sixteenth century, and their belief that the use of systems similar to the repartimiento for drafting agricultural labor at the end of the seventeenth century represented a new development rather than continuing application of a system which had never been entirely abandoned.

[104] Velasco II to the king, Mexico City, April 6, 1594, MS in AGI, 58–3–12 (BLT), states only 8 per cent at the two peak seasons, but the documents in Zavala and Castelo, *op. cit.*, I–V, *passim*, point to 10 per cent as the usual peak season quota.

[105] Instrucción que ha de guardar Alonso de Medina Quiros en el repartimiento de los Indios de las minas de Çimapan, Mexico City, May 28, 1599, in Zavala and Castelo, *op. cit.*, IV, 271–274, is an example of the standard instruction embodying these provisions. The discrepancy between the much higher percentage of the males which this instruction would have recruited and the rate of 4 per cent without extra levy assessed for mine service is explained by the exemption of Indian nobles and public officials from service which cut down the yield by approximately a fifth.

[106] Memorial of Villamanrrique to the king, n.d. but *ante* 1590, MS in AGI, 58–3–11 (BLT).

[107] Instruction to Agustín Manuel Pimentel, *juez comisario de los alquileres de Tulancingo,* Mexico City, September 4, 1606, in Zavala and Castelo, *op. cit.*, VI, 41–46. This was a form instruction.

[108] Velasco II to the king, Mexico City, April 6, 1594, MS in AGI, 58–3–12 (BLT); Copia de los advertimientos que el Virrey don Luis de Velasco dexó al Conde de monteRey para el gouierno de la nueua España, *ca.* November, 1595, MS in AGI, 58–3–13 (BLT); Zavala and Castelo, *op. cit.*, introductions to Vols. IV–VI *et passim*. A typical reassessment is the order of the Conde de Coruña to the corregidor of Otumba, Mexico City, February 9, 1583, MS in AGN, Indios, II, fol. 114ᵛ (BLT).

[109] Zavala and Castelo, *op. cit.*, introductions to Vols. IV–VIII, which although intended to show the effectiveness of the royal legislation actually demonstrate the reverse.

[110] *Recopilación de Castilla,* Lib. V, Tít. XVI, ley IV, *Tomo Primero [segundo] de los leyes de recopilación [y tomo tercero de autos acordados]* (3 vols., Madrid, 1782) I, 783.

[111] Zavala and Castelo, *op. cit.*, introductions to Vols. III–VIII, use the term *gañán* for free wage laborer, but this term in the seventeenth century, as now, applied only to agricultural workers. See Francisco Javier Santamaría, *Diccionario general de americanismos* (3 vols., Mexico City, 1942–[1943]) and Real Academia Española, *Diccionario de la lengua española* (2d. printing of 16th ed., Madrid, 1939) on *gañán, naboria, peón,* etc. The discussion of *naboria* in these dictionaries is badly in error. See also Simpson, *The Encomienda,* pp. 22 and 178, n. 15, and John Horace Parry, *The Audiencia of New Galicia in the Sixteenth Century. A Study in Spanish Colonial Government* (Cambridge, England, Cambridge University Press, 1948), pp. 51, 56–57.

[112] Royal cédula of the king to the Audiencia of Mexico, Madrid, June 20, 1567, and Act of Obedience, Mexico City, October 5, 1567, MS in AGN, Reales cédulas, duplicados, XLVII, fols. 339ᵛ–340ᵛ (BLT). Montemayor y Córdova de Cuenca, Pt. II, auto 93, lists a cédula on the same subject dated Madrid, June 20, 1576, nine years later than the cédula of 1567 to the day. For this reason the date in Montemayor may be a transposition. At any rate, the cédula he lists was implemented in May, 1586 by an *auto acordado* of the Audiencia of Mexico.

Kubler, *Mexican Architecture of the Sixteenth Century*, I, 144, cites evidence that debt peonage was fairly well established as early as 1575. Zavala and Castelo, *op. cit.*, III, vi–xiii, discuss free wage labor so-called as a phenomenon existing in the period 1584–1591 but consider it relatively unimportant. For interesting notations of two documents of October 9, 1571 and January 30, 1574, pointing to the use of debt to secure Indians for labor in the mines of Tasco, see Zavala and Castelo, *op. cit.*, I, 1–3.

[113] Relación del estado que tienen las haziendas de minas de la nueua hespaña y de lo que a su magestad deuen procedido de açogues sacada de la visita general que de las dichas minas se hizo por principio del año passado de 97., n.d. but early 1598, MS in AGI, 58-3-13 (BLT).

[114] *Ca.* 1603, according to Mota y Escobar, *op. cit.*, p. 134.

[115] Zavala and Castelo, *op. cit.*, III, vi–xiii, hold to the contrary opinion that the repartimiento became the principal means of supplying Indian labor at the end of the sixteenth century. However, their own discussion (Vol. IV, xii-xvi) and the documents in Vols. III and IV make clear the existence of a substantial amount of debt peonage in agriculture as well as mining by the end of the sixteenth century.

[116] Under the repartimiento in its later development, by directly providing food; under debt peonage, either by providing food or by allowing time and land for the Indians to raise their own.

[117] Zavala, *op. cit.*, p. 317; Copia de los advertimientos que el Virrey don Luis de Velasco dexó al Conde de monteRey para el gouierno de la nueua España, *ca.* November, 1595, MS in AGI, 58-3-13 (BLT); royal cédula of November 24, 1601, Valladolid, in Zavala and Castelo, *op. cit.*, V, vi–xi; royal cédula of May 26, 1609, Aranjuez, in Simpson, *The Repartimiento System*, pp. 129–140.

[118] Royal letter of June 4, 1582, Lisbon, ordered implemented by the Conde de Coruña, November 28, 1582. These are cited in two viceregal confirmations for the mines of Pachuca and Temascaltepec, Mexico City, November 22, 1603 and February 22, 1604, respectively, in Zavala and Castelo, *op. cit.*, V, 160–161, 245–246, respectively. See in the same work Vol. VI, xxxviii.

[119] See cédula of June 20, 1567, Madrid, cited in note 112; order of Velasco II to the alcalde mayor of Texcoco, Mexico City, March 29, 1591; order of Monterrey on the naborios of Anton Pintón, Chapultepec, August 12, 1600 (this cites previous orders of 1584 and 1586); order of Monterrey on Indian naborios of San Luis Potosí, Mexico City, October 9, 1602; order of Monterrey, Mexico City, August 22, 1603; order of Montesclaros, Mexico City, December 5, 1603; orders of Montesclaros, Mexico City, November 15, 16, 1606; in Zavala and Castelo, *op. cit.*, III, 162–163; IV, 453; V, 44–45, 108, 167–168; VI, 86–87 respectively; ordinance of Marqués de Guadalcázar confirming previous ones of 1611 and 1612, April 30, 1614, MS in AGN, Ordenanzas, I, fols. 164ᵛ–166ᵛ (BLT). By 1603 the issuing of orders for return of fugitives from debt labor had become so standardized that the orders begin to bear the notation "*el ordinario ...*" or " "*el mandamiento ordinario.*" See also Montemayor y Córdova de Cuenca, *op. cit.*, Pt. III, ordinance 48.

[120] Cédula of the king to the Audiencia of Mexico, Madrid, June 20, 1567, MS in AGN, Reales cédulas, duplicados, XLVII, fols. 339–340 (BLT); order of Monterrey on naborios employed at San Luis Potosí, Mexico City, October 9, 1602 (this cites ordinances of March 26, 1598 and September 15, 1597), in Zavala and Castelo, *op. cit.*, V, 44–45; order of Monterrey on the use of force, etc. by the Spanish of the mines of San Luis and Sichu, Mexico City, August 30, 1599, in Zavala and Castelo, *op. cit.*, IV, 324–325; order of Guadalcázar forbidding advances of any kind to Indians, Mexico City, May 15, 1619, in Zavala and Castelo, *op. cit.*, VI, 372–373; Montemayor y Córdova de Cuenca, *op. cit.*, Pt. II, autos 93, 97, and 98, Pt. III, ordinance 48. See the discussion in Zavala and Castelo, *op. cit.*, IV, xii–xvi; VI, ix–x, xxiv–xxvi;

VII, x–xii; VIII, vii–x, and Zavala, *op. cit.,* pp. 330–340. Zavala and Castelo hold that the famous ordinance of Palafox y Mendoza of August 19, 1642 (*op. cit.,* VII, 457–460) did away with all restrictions on the amount of money that might be loaned, since no restriction is mentioned in it. In the light of subsequent viceregal ordinances discussed by the two authors, it seems more likely that Palafox y Mendoza merely reiterated the existing rule without any change, the limitations being understood.

[121] Relacion de los mandamientos que se han despachado los años pasados para las minas de Tasco, en el oficio del Secretario Juan de Cueva y refrendados de él, [refers to orders of 1571–1574] in Zavala and Castelo, *op. cit.,* I, 1–3; order of Palafox y Mendoza as *visitador-general* on the laborers of the Spanish farmers of Huejotzingo, Puebla, June 10, 1641, repeated in his general ordinance of August 19, 1642, Mexico City, in Zavala and Castelo, *op. cit.,* VII, 457–460; *ibid.,* VI, xxxvii; VII, x–xii; VIII, xii–xviii; Zavala, *op. cit.,* pp. 340–348.

[122] License of the Conde de Monterrey for sale of the *obraje* of Melchor Alvarez, vecino de Puebla, Mexico City, January 14, 1600, in Zavala and Castelo, *op. cit.,* IV, 387–388; *ibid.,* VII, xv–xvi and VIII, xii–xviii; Zavala, *op. cit.,* pp. 341–345.

[123] Zavala and Castelo, *op. cit.,* VI, xxvi–xxxvii. Order of Palafox y Mendoza as visitador-general on the laborers of the Spanish farmers of Huejotzingo, Puebla, June 10, 1641, in *ibid.,* VII, 457–460.

[124] *Ibid.,* introductions to Vols. VI, VII, VIII.

[125] Order of the Marqués de Cerralvo cancelling commissions for all *jueces repartidores* save for mines after January 1, 1633, Mexico City, December 31, 1632, in Zavala and Castelo, *op. cit.,* VI, 615–624.

[126] Zavala and Castelo, *op. cit.,* VII, xii–ix, xvii–xix; VIII, xviii–lii; Simpson, *The Repartimiento System,* pp. 44–45.

[127] See order of Marqués de Villena to the justices of the villas of San Miguel and San Felipe, October 30, 1640, in Zavala and Castelo, *op. cit.,* VI, 615–624. See also *ibid.,* supp. VII, vii–ix.

[128] Order of the Conde de Montezuma to the alcalde mayor of Metepec, Mexico City, August 18, 1699, and order of the Duque de Alburquerque, confirming an order of the Conde de Galve, Mexico City, April 28, 1708, in Zavala and Castelo, *op. cit.,* VIII, 123–124 and 171–172 respectively. See also in the same volume, pp. x–xi; Zavala, *op. cit.,* pp. 328–329.

[129] Zavala and Castelo, *op. cit.,* VII, xvii, and VIII, xvii.

[130] *Ibid.,* VI, xxix, and VII, xxviii–xxix.

[131] "A Relation of the Transactions of the Vera Cruz Factory whilst under the Management of David Findlay and William Butler," London, May 3, 1736, in Elizabeth Donnan, ed., *Documents Illustrative of the History of the Slave Trade to America* (Publication 409 of the Carnegie Institution of Washington, 4 vols., Washington, D.C., 1930–1935) II, 458–459.

[132] Zavala and Castelo, *op. cit.,* IV, xii–xiii; VI, xii–xiii, xxvi–xxvii; VII, xii–xv.

[133] Memorial of Villamanrrique to the king, n.d. but *ante* 1590, MS in AGI, 58–3–11 (BLT); Velasco II to the Council of the Indies on proposals of the Junta de la Contaduría, n.d., MS in AGI, 58–3–11 (BLT); Relación del estado que tienen las haziendas de minas de la nueua hespaña y de lo que a su magestad deuen procedido de açogues sacada de la visita general que de las dichas minas se hizo por principio del año pasado de 97, n.d. but early 1598, MS in AGI, 58–3–13 (BLT); [Monterrey] Advertimientos que ha parescido embiar a Vuestra Magestad Sobre el estado pressente de la real hazienda desta nueua hespaña ... ,Mexico City, April 1, 1598, MS in AGI, 58–3–13 (BLT); Mota y Escobar, *op. cit.,* pp. 138–143. See also West, *op. cit.,* pp. 15–43 for a careful description of Mexican mining in the colonial period and Humboldt, *op. cit.* III, 371–372. Francisco de Urdiñola blamed part of the threatened drop in mining output on the fact that wealthy miners customarily bought out smaller ones to gain exclusive or nearly exclusive control of a mining *real.* The new owners were unable, or did not choose, to work all of their claims. The letter is especially notable in that Urdiñola listed himself as one of the culprits. Letter to the king, Durango, March 31, 1604, MS in AGI, 66–6–17 (BLT).

[134] See pp. 1–2. The statement on the rhythm of mining production in this study is based on the figures in Earl J. Hamilton, "Imports of American Gold and Silver into Spain, 1503–1660," *The Quarterly Journal of Economics,* XLIII (May, 1929), 436–472, and *American*

Treasure and the Price Revolution in Spain, 1501–1650 . . . (Cambridge, Mass., Harvard University Press, 1934) pp. 34–43. Although Hamilton's figures deal only with receipts of specie through legal channels in Spain, they offer the best clue available not to specific figures of output but to relative movement of production. Export of specie to the Philippines, retention in New Spain, and smuggling alone cannot account for the sharp drop in receipts of specie in Spain in the middle decades of the sixteenth century. Moreover, New Spain, with its few good harbors and much more easily watched coastline, probably offered less opportunity for smuggling and foreign interloping than did the viceroyalty of Peru with its backdoor route to Buenos Aires. The drop in receipts indicated by Hamilton—nearly 90 per cent of the peak by 1656–1660— must have been in large measure the effect of decrease in output.

[125] Humboldt, *op. cit.*, IV, 101–104.